A Psychometrics Primer

D0861120

A Psychometrics Primer

Paul Kline

FREE ASSOCIATION BOOKS / LONDON / NEW YORK

First published in Great Britain in 2000 by
FREE ASSOCIATION BOOKS
57 Warren Street
London W1T 5NR

www.fabooks.com

A CIP catalogue record for this book is available
from the British Library.

ISBN 1 85343 489 2 pbk

10 9 8 7 6 5 4 3

Produced for the publisher by
Chase Publishing Services Ltd, Sidmouth
Printed and bound in the European Union by
Antony Rowe Ltd, Chippenham and Eastbourne, England

Contents

1
What is Psychometrics?

The literal, etymological meaning of psychometrics, measuring the soul, indicates quite clearly what it is. Psychometrics refers to all those aspects of psychology which are concerned with psychological testing, both the methods of testing and the substantive findings. It can be thought of, indeed, as the study of individual differences. That is why psychometrics is anathema to those of egalitarian persuasion. Of course, this means little without some indication of the nature of psychological testing and this is set out below.

Types of Psychological Test

A simple way of gaining some insight into psychological testing is to set out different types of psychological test. This, needless to say, assumes that the tests are valid, that is that they really measure what they claim to measure. Although, as we shall discuss throughout this book, there is much dispute on exactly this point, for our present argument we shall assume that psychological tests are valid.

Intelligence Tests

One of the first psychological tests was the intelligence test. Such a measure was devised by Binet and Simon (Binet and Simon, 1905) and this very test, in a highly developed form, is still in use. Intelligence, as measured by psychometric intelligence tests, refers to a basic reasoning ability which appears to be common to many different intellectual tasks. This is a controversial subject and it is to be regretted that much of the discussion is not well informed. However, it is fully discussed in Chapter 5 and in much more detail in Kline (1991) and comprehensively in Jensen (1998). Today intelligence tests are widely used in educational psychology and in job selection. Of all the different kinds of psychometric tests intelligence tests are the most effective and valid. Thus, in brief, we can see that the measurement of reasoning ability is one aspect of psychometric testing.

Ability tests

In addition to intelligence, it is clear, from the study of human performance, that there are other abilities of a more specialised nature. This is not at all surprising in the light of human experience, although this is often ignored in some branches of academic psychology. For example, it makes sense to think of writers and physicists as being both of above average intelligence, the former high on verbal ability, the latter on mathematical ability. In fact the study of human abilities (the results of which are described in Chapter 5) using the special statistical methods of psychometrics (notably factor analysis, described in Chapter 4) has shown that there are many special abilities of which the most important are verbal ability, spatial ability and mathematical reasoning. Indeed in psychometrics there is an agreement on what these abilities are, which is unusual in psychology. A full account can be found in Carroll (1993).

Personality Tests

While the psychometric testing of human abilities fits well with our experience, since most people are made aware of individual differences almost as soon as they start school, personality testing is by no means so obvious. In fact one of the most difficult and intransigent problems in psychometrics concerns the definition of personality. It is by now a truism of textbooks in psychology that there are as many definitions of personality as there are psychologists attempting to define it. From the viewpoint of psychometrics a working definition of personality is that it represents the total of all variables, other than those of ability, on which individuals differ. This is essentially the definition used by Cattell (for example, 1957) as a basis for his pioneering studies of individual differences in personality. The aim of psychometrics is, therefore, to discover and study the most important variables giving rise to such differences in personality. Actually this definition of personality also includes motivational and mood variables but these may be distinguished quite easily. Personality traits are stable and of long duration while moods and states (such as anger and fatigue) are transient; personality traits (sometimes referred to as temperamental traits) refer to how we do what we do while motivational states are dynamic, referring to why we do what we do. Personality tests are described in detail in Chapter 6 and it is sufficient here to point out that there are three types of personality tests.

Personality Questionnaires

These consist of lists of questions and statements about behaviour and subjects have to indicate whether these are true for them or apply to them. Typical examples are: 'Do you sleep well in hot weather?' and 'I always shut the window at night.' Such questionnaires or inventories are accurate to score, easy to administer and are much favoured by applied psychologists, especially for selection (see Chapter 8).

Projective Tests

The essence of the projective test is the presentation to subjects of ambiguous stimuli which they have to describe. A famous example is the inkblot test devised by Rorschach (1921). The point of the ambiguity is that this compels, according to projective test theory, subjects to project something of themselves into their description. It is this which is analysed by the tester. Objectors to projective testing, of which there are many, argue that this interpretative act is too subjective and imprecise for any scientific measurement. These problems are discussed in Chapter 6.

Objective Tests

Objective tests, sometimes called performance tests (for example, Cronbach, 1984), are the third variety of personality test, although they are far less widely used than those which I have described. In fact they are largely experimental in nature. Cattell (Cattell and Warburton, 1967) defined a test as objective if it could be objectively scored, that is if the scoring system was such that there was no room for disagreement, and if its meaning could not be guessed by subjects. This second feature was designed to obviate an obvious objection to questionnaire items, namely that they are so easy to fake. Thus, for example, if one went for a job as a salesperson, it would be absurd to answer the item 'Are you afraid to talk to people?' with 'Yes', and few applicants do. In fact any task which is opaque to subjects and which yields individual differences might be used as an objective personality test. However, the problem here lies in establishing what such tests measure. All these difficulties are discussed in Chapter 6.

Motivational Tests

As was mentioned in the previous paragraph, motivational tests are distinguished from personality tests because the former deal with the dynamics of behaviour. The attempt to measure the variables which cause our actions. Tests of this kind, which are discussed in Chapter 7, are much less well developed than tests of ability and personality. This is partly because in psychology there is no well-agreed theory concerning what ought to be measured. As a consequence of this there is a large variety of tests which might loosely be described as motivational. These measure: moods, such as anger or fear; interests, such as clerical or people; more specific interests related to particular jobs, useful for selection; and, as a final example, more theoretically based underlying dynamic variables such as the sex drive and self-sentiment.

Other Tests

In addition to the psychological tests which have been constructed to measure ability, personality and motivation, specialised tests have been developed for particular applications, often in clinical and medical psychology. In this book we shall not deal in detail with such measures although a brief discussion of them can be found in Chapter 7.

Form this it is clear that psychometrics is concerned with the measurement of all aspects of human psychology, not just behaviour but in some cases variables believed to account for behaviour.

Why Measurement is Important in Psychology

There can be no doubt that the natural sciences have enormously increased the fund of knowledge in the world. Their success is due in a large part to the use of the scientific method which has been subjected to considerable philosophical analysis of which the work of Popper (1959) is a good illustration. An essential component of the scientific method, in most fields of science, is precise measurement. Precise measurement allows precise testing of hypotheses. The language of mathematics cannot be fudged. Thus psychometrists have argued (for example, Cattell, 1981 and Eysenck, 1986) that good psychological measurement is essential for a scientific psychology and this is the aim of psychometrics: to provide precise measurement of psychological variables as a basis for a scientific psychology. Without such a basis of good measurement psychology quickly retreats into a morass of verbiage, unclear, opinion rather than knowledge in the Platonic sense of those terms, unable to distinguish between truth and fiction, driven by political rectitude, a hermeneutics out of touch with reality, such as may be seen in the social sciences.

Of course it is possible, in principle, that the nature of the subject matter of psychology is such that it defeats good measurement. Measuring length or mass is, prima facie, different from measuring mental processes or emotions and these arguments which are fundamental to psychometrics will be discussed in Chapter 2.

How Psychometrics is Used in Psychology

Although precise measurement is necessary for science it is not sufficient. Once the measurements have been made something needs to be done with the results. There are really three aspects to psychometrics which I shall mention before bringing this introductory chapter to a close.

Methodological

It is not a simple matter to measure psychological variables. Over the approximately 100 years of its existence psychometrics has developed some extremely powerful and sophisticated statistical procedures in an effort to improve measurement. This is particularly the case since the advent of high-speed computers, which have rendered possible methods which previously could only be conceived. In Chapter 4 what are generally considered the best methods will be described as simply as possible, with the minimum of mathematics, the aim of this section being to confer understanding of the psychometric principles. However, it must be realised that many psychometricians are involved in the improvement and development of statistical methods and it is only from such painstaking research that precise measurements can be made.

Applied Psychometrics

Research into psychometric methods of the kind described in the previous paragraph demands a statistical and mathematical expertise which is beyond that of most psychologists and many psychometrists. In fact it is the resort of a minority of specialists. The majority of psychometrists are interested in the practical applications of psychometrics and these are fully discussed in Chapter 8. A few examples will clarify how psychometrics is applied and I shall take them from the main branches of applied psychometrics.

Educational Psychology

In educational psychology the psychologists may be asked to account for the poor progress of a particular pupil. Here an intelligence test is a most useful measure. If the child is highly intelligent it is clear that other factors must be interfering with her educational progress. If, on the other hand, she turns out to be of below average intelligence, it may be that too much is expected of her. Similarly for younger children there are diagnostic tests which can pinpoint specific problems in, say, reading or arithmetic, and this can be valuable for the teacher.

Occupational Psychology

There are two common tasks for the occupational psychologist: selection and career development, and for both of these psychometric tests are valuable. In the former, tests will be used which are known to correlate with success at the job involved. It is interesting to note in this respect that the single best predictor for any job is the intelligence test (Ghiselli, 1966). For career development the psychologist builds up a picture of the individual which is discussed with her in the light of current and future job opportunities.

Clinical Psychology

Here tests can be used to aid diagnosis and monitor treatment. A good example of this is acquired aphasia (inability to speak) which occurs after a stroke or other vascular accident. Aphasic tests are useful for discovering exactly what aspects of language understanding and expression have been lost. The most recent edition of the *Aphasic Screening Test* (Whurr, 1996) illustrates this typical clinical application of psychometrics.

Theoretical Psychometrics

It was argued previously that the aim of psychometrics was to provide the precise measurement required for psychology to become a natural science. This has been the aim of my psychometric work since I was trained in psychometrics in the London School which pioneered the factor analysis of human abilities (Spearman, 1904) and continued through Burt, Eysenck and Cattell with whom I had the good fortune to work. It was their hope that the factor analysis of ability and personality would lead to the isolation of the fundamental variables underlying human behaviour. These could then be studied with the scientific aim of understanding and predicting human behaviour and producing a quantitative account. This is a lofty ideal which has not been realised, perhaps because standards of measurement in psychometrics were not as robust as they are in the natural sciences, a topic which I shall deal with in Chapter 2. However, thanks to the work of measurement theorists (for example, Michell, 1990) these defects may be remedied as I have fully discussed elsewhere (Kline, 1998, 1999).

Conclusions

The conclusions to this introductory chapter on the nature of psychometrics can be brief. I have shown that psychometrics is concerned with psychological testing and that tests have been devised to measure human abilities, personality and motivation. Precise measurement, it was argued, is an essential of the scientific method and a necessity if psychology is to emerge from the slough of the social sciences. It turns out that there are three aspects to psychometrics: the development of statistical methods, the application of psychometric tests especially in clincal, occupational and educational psychology, and the development of quantitative psychological theory.

All this, the subject of psychometrics, will be described and scrutinised in this *Psychometrics Primer* and we begin, in Chapter 2, with the study of what constitutes scientific measurement.

2
Scientific Measurement

In Chapter 1 it was pointed out that the great advances in knowledge which we have seen in the natural sciences have been attributed to the use, in those subjects, of the scientific method. Critical features of the scientific method are its insistence on testing hypotheses and precise measurement. This latter is an integral aspect of the former. Indeed it is the precision of the sciences and their reliance on quantification which are their hallmark.

It is just these features which distinguish science from other disciplines, and in psychology this is particularly important because psychology, from the nature of its subject matter, is often studied by methods far different from those in the natural sciences, as a few examples will illustrate.

Psychologists are often confused with psychoanalysts. Psychoanalysts, who may utilise the theories of Freud, Jung and Lacan amongst countless others, concern themselves with psychological matters but are not in any way scientific. For example, they argue that the basis of neurosis resides in the Oedipus complex (Freud, 1933). Since they use no measures of neurosis or Oedipus complex, such hypotheses are difficult to test. Thus they are not science but dogma, assertions based upon, they claim, the free associations of patients, data which cannot be refuted, although Freudian theories at least can be restated in a testable form, as has been shown by Kline (1981).

Similarly much current social psychology, especially that of the social constructionists, is profoundly anti-scientific. It argues in the case of personality that this is itself a social construction and is not open to objective verification (Burr, 1995). This is the conceptual basis for qualitative assessment, which is now taught as part of the scientific method in psychology (a development which strains the credulity of this writer, and shows how the notion of science in psychology has been diluted). All this is quite hopeless and one of the aims of psychometrics is to avoid these scientifically valueless speculations and replace them with theories based upon rigorously measured data. However, to understand how this may be done it is necessary to examine the nature of measurement in the natural sciences.

The Nature of Scientific Measurement

Although the nature of scientific measurement intuitively seems to be a straightforward matter it turns out that this is far from the case. It is, in fact, precisely this complexity as to what constitutes good, scientific measurement which has allowed much of the confusion concerning psychometric measurement, a confusion which will be examined as this chapter proceeds.

It is fortunate, therefore, that recently these difficult problems of measurement have been clarified from a theoretical viewpoint by Michell (1990, 1997) whose work formed a starting point for a study of how these difficulties should be dealt with in psychometrics – *The New Psychometrics* (Kline, 1998). A summary of this new approach to psychometrics, based upon measurement theory, can be found in Chapter 9.

There are two critical aspects to scientific measurement according to Michell (1997) and these are set out below.

The Definition

Scientific measurement is defined as 'the estimation or discovery of the relation of some magnitude of a quantitative unit to a unit of the same attribute'. If an attribute has a quantitative structure then it is a mathematical theorem that magnitudes of a quantity stand in numerical relations, one to another. The task of scientific measurement is to discover or estimate these relations. As Michell (1990) argues, this is the basic logic of scientific measurement.

Quantitative Structure

There is no logical necessity that any attribute be quantitative. That it be so is an hypothesis, open to empirical verification. It is necessary, therefore, to demonstrate by means of empirical evidence that an attribute possesses quantitative structure. Thus this is the second task (which strictly should be prior to measurement itself), for scientific measurement to demonstrate that the attribute is quantitative. Clearly it is literally nonsensical to attempt to measure some variable which is not in fact quantitative. This particular difficulty is usually referred to as the representational problem since, if measurement is to be meaningful, the measurements must represent some relationship in the real world (Coombs et al., 1970).

Both these defining characteristics of scientific measurement have been expressed in rather abstract terms and in a condensed form. I shall expand them and clarify them with some illustrations. Some attributes, quantities, are measurable, that is they have a quantitative structure. Length is one of the clearest examples. Magnitudes, which are specific instances of a quantity, are measurable because they stand in ratios one to another, on account of this quantitative structure. Indeed, Michell (1997) demonstrates that if an attribute has quantitative structure, then for any two magnitudes, a and b, the ratio of a and b, is the measure of a in units of b. This is why, as argued above, scientific measurement demands that we discover the additive structure of the attribute in order to discover the ratios between magnitudes.

Length clearly exemplifies the nature of scientific measurement. First, there is no doubt that length has a quantitative structure. We can measure the length of an object with a set of measuring rods. The concatenation of these, perhaps a metre long, to measure, say, a wall of 5 metres length makes it obvious that length has an additive structure. Such measurement is known as extensive or fundamental measurement. The mathematical *proof* of quantitative structure (as distinct from intuitive illustration) is, in fact, highly complex and readers must be referred to Michell (1990).

Given this structure, the measurement of length beautifully illustrates the other characteristics of scientific measurement.

Units of Measurement

In my opinion this is the key characteristic of scientific measurement. In the case of length we can have various units, metres, inches, miles. Units of measurement are critical for a number of different reasons.

Accuracy

In scientific measurement these units allow enormous accuracy, defining accuracy as agreement with some benchmark measure. In the case of length originally there was a perfect metre rule in Sèvres, as also there was a perfect kilogram. Now, however, the base units are defined in terms of fundamental properties of matter. A metre is now defined by the length travelled by light in a vacuum in a given amount of time, although the perfect kilogram is still in use. Thus units of measurement allow but do not guarantee a high degree of accuracy.

Meaningfulness of Measurements

In most cases units of measurement make it absolutely clear what is being measured. If I have a ruler there can be no argument, other than by the insane, as to what I am measuring. A ruler unequivocally measures length. There could be no plausible case made that it measured voltage, temperature or pressure. It is important to note that the meaningfulness of units is often attested by their theoretical benchmark: the Kelvin, the unit of measurement of temperature, reflects the behaviour of water at various temperatures. Similarly many of the other measures in the natural sciences have units of measurement which are a part of the theoretical structure of those sciences. Again the units are quite unequivocal in meaning. For example, the measurement of electric current, the ampere, or the measurement of electrical potential, the volt. These units of measurement being unequivocal add to the clarity of science.

Base Units and Derived Units

This last example from electricity illustrates a further important aspect of units of measurement. As has been made clear, units of measurement entail meaningful measurement. However, there are two kinds of units of measurement: base units and derived units. Length, in terms of metres, and time, in terms of seconds, are examples of base units and these are precisely defined. The ampere is one such base unit. Derived units involve some relationship between base units, and in the natural sciences, the majority of measurements use derived units of measurement. Examples of these are: density, in which the measure is kilograms per cubic metre; velocity, metres per second; and magnetic field, which is defined as amperes per metre. In summary, therefore, it can be seen that in the natural sciences measurement is carried out in terms of specified units of measurement, base units or derived units which are themselves made up from the base units. These give meaning to all the measurements.

The Ratios of Measurement

As has been argued measurement entails the discovery or estimation of the relation of some magnitude of a quantitative unit to a unit of the same attribute. Clearly without units of measurement such a definition cannot be met, or, in other words, scientific measurement is impossible. An illustration of such a ratio, given by Michell (1997), is the measurement of a cricket pitch: the ratio is 22 to the unit of a yard. Such measurements yield what are known as ratio scales which have equal intervals and true zeros. These ratio scales are fully discussed later in this chapter, in relation to psychometric tests. Here, however, it is sufficient to mention briefly why equal intervals and true zeros are important aspects of scientific measurement. Having a true zero gives meaning to measurement provided the size of the intervals or units of measurement is known. With a true zero a measurement of 1 is meaningful, although this meaning differs depending upon whether the unit is a millimetre, a metre or a mile. The possession of equal intervals is vital for many computational procedures, as will be discussed later in this section. What it means is simply illustrated. The difference between 9 and 10 metres is exactly the same as that between 1 and 2 metres and all through the scale.

Equivalence of Units

There is another aspect to having clear units of measurement which also gives one confidence that measurement is accurate. This was exemplified in our illustration of the meaning of equal intervals. It makes absolutely no difference, except as a matter of convenience and practicality, to our measurements whether we use millimetres, centimetres or miles. All results are equivalent.

Quantitative Structure

It was pointed out in the opening section on the nature of scientific measurement that there was no necessity that any attribute did have quantitative structure. If it did not, measurement was meaningless and thus it was an important aspect of scientific measurement to demonstrate quantitative structure. Length is probably one of the clearest possible illustrations of such structure. However, two further points need to be made. The first concerns the demonstration of quantitative structure. In fact this is a complex matter of measurement theory which goes beyond the scope of this Primer. It is sufficient to note that sometimes, as in the measure of density, the quantitative structure of the attribute is not based upon simple concatenation. Thus objects of different densities when combined do not yield an object of a density which is the sum of their densities. This is different from combining two lines. Density, of course, is a derived unit of measurement – from two variables, mass and volume. For a more detailed discussion readers must be referred to Michell (1990, 1997) or Kline (1998). The second point concerns conjoint measurement which I discuss below.

Conjoint Measurement

This is another highly complex topic which was first developed by Luce and Tukey (1964), and was so difficult mathematically that it never received the attention it deserved from most psychometrists. This was particularly unfortunate because it is of particular relevance to psychological measurement. However, in Chapter 4 I shall describe this form of measurement in a comprehensible fashion. As Gregory (1997) argues and demonstrates it is possible to explicate complex mathematical arguments without mathematics, 'handwaving' in his terminology. Conjoint measurement is exemplified in the case where a response to a test item is clearly a function of just two variables, for example, item difficulty and subject's ability, as, perhaps, in an intelligence test. Luce and Tukey (1964) proved that in such a case there is quantitative structure. Brilliant as this may be there remains the difficulty of showing that just two variables can account for the measurements.

Assuming Quantitative Structure

Although Michell (1997) convincingly argued that whether an attribute possesses quantitative structure is a matter of fact and thus evidence is required, this evidence is not easy to obtain. Jensen (1980), in the light of such difficulties, has argued that, to take intelligence as an example, it makes sense to assume quantitative structure for as long as our measurements make sense in the real world and, in this instance, they do (see Chapter 5). This seems a sensible scientific procedure but in many instances of psychological measurement there are no such convincing results.

Conclusions Concerning the Nature of Scientific Measurement

From this discussion some general points can be made which summarise the argument so far.

- Units of measurement. In the natural sciences there are usually clear and meaningful units of measurement: base units, such as metres and seconds, and derived units, such as velocity, metres per second.
- Quantitative structure. For measurement to make sense, it is necessary to demonstrate that the attribute to be measured has quantitative structure, although this is not a simple matter so to do.
- Ratio scales. Scientific measurement by definition demands ratio scales for it is the discovery or estimation of the ratio of a unit of measurement to a magnitude of the same attribute, a metre to the height of a mountain. Ratio scales have equal intervals and true zeros.

The Nature of Psychometric Measurement

Having explicated the nature of scientific measurement, I shall now examine the essence of psychometric measurement in order to see to what extent, if any, it differs from measurement in the natural sciences. From the nature of the subject matter of psychology, compared with the natural sciences, it could well be that psychometric measurement differed considerably from that in the sciences yet still retained those features which we have seen to be critical to it.

Michell (1997) has a succinct account of the nature of psychometric testing which I shall summarise and develop where it is required although it must be pointed out that Michell would not necessarily endorse all the argument which I set out below.

The Attributes or Variables to be Measured

As was pointed out in Chapter 1, psychometric testing is concerned with the measurement of ability, personality and motivation. These are the three broad areas of psychometric testing. Within each area the variables measured are particular traits: intelligence and spatial ability typifying abilities, extraversion and authoritarianism being examples of personality. There are several points about these variables which must be noted here, which make their measurement different from that of the natural sciences.

Definition of Variables

In the natural sciences the variables to be measured are not disputed. There is no question as to the nature of velocity, length or density, to use the examples which were discussed in the previous section. This is simply not the case with psychological variables. Often, and this will be scrutinised at various junctures in this book, the attribute is defined by the test itself. Thus intelligence is what intelligence tests measure (Boring, 1923). This merely turns the problem into one of defining what intelligence tests measure although, as shall be seen in Chapter 5, this can be done quite effectively. However, it must be noted that some psychologists argue for the notion of not one but multiple intelligences (for example, Gardner, 1983) and a few regard the concept as redundant, although this would appear to be entirely mistaken. The point here is that intelligence is the variable about which there is most agreement in psychometrics! In respect of personality and motivational variables there are, indeed, endless disputes, as can be seen from a scrutiny of Saklofske and Zeidner (1995). Thus in this vital issue of knowing what is being measured there is a considerable gulf between psychometrics and scientific measurement.

Quantitative Structure

This can be dealt with briefly since it was fully discussed with relation to intelligence in the previous section. However, as Michell (1997) argues, the need to demonstrate quantitative structure is usually ignored. If it is not then it is assumed, as was the case with Jensen (1980). This is a serious flaw since such quantitative structure underlies the measurement in the first place. The meaning of any numbers where there is no such structure is problematic. This point will be amplified in our discussion, later in this chapter, of different types of scale. It is certainly a strange procedure to attempt to develop a measure of an attribute which is not quantitative.

Definition of Measurement

As Michell (1997) demonstrated, a survey of psychometric and psychology texts showed that there was a virtually universal definition of psychological measurement of which the essence is: the assignment of numerals to objects or events, according to a rule. By objects or events writers usually mean the common set of psychological variables, such as intelligence, aggression, anxiety and so on. This follows the work of Stevens (1946) which has been almost entirely accepted in psychology. There are important issues raised by this definition of measurement and these are set out below.

Comparison with the Definition of Scientific Measurement

Scientific measurement was defined as the estimation or discovery of the ratio of a unit of measurement to another magnitude of the same attribute. Thus the definition of psychological measurement as the assignment of numbers by some rule is entirely different. There is no overlap between these definitions. On definition alone one would be forced to include that psychological measurement was not scientific.

✦ No Units of Measurement

As is obvious from the definition there are no units of measurement implicit in this definition of psychological measurement. The resulting lack of clarity and accuracy has been mentioned previously.

✦ No Ratio Scales

With no units of measurement ratio scales with true zeros are not possible. The full implications of this will be discussed later in this chapter.

Assignment of Numbers by Rules

There is an obvious difficulty here. How are the rules devised? It is clearly possible to devise an absurd rule to assign numbers to some trait, which everybody would deem unacceptable. However, this raises the issue of what is acceptable. When we say acceptable it must imply that it fits with reality, but how do we know what this reality is, which the rules must fit. Assignment of numbers by some rule is not, in itself, a satisfactory account of measurement.

Conclusions

This comparison of scientific and psychological measurement makes it clear that psychological measurement is simply in a different category. It resembles scientific measurement in no particular other than that both types are numerical. Critically psychological measurement has no units of measurement, its assignment of numbers is rule-bound but arbitrary and not necessarily linked to the nature of the attribute to be measured.

The obvious conclusion is that psychological and thus psychometric measurement is not scientific. However, this would be denied by most psychometrists and thus it is necessary to summarise the arguments by which Stevens (1946) defended his definition of measurement.

Stevens' Definition of Psychological Measurement

This has been fully scrutinised by Michell (1990, 1997) and by Kline (1998). Here I shall summarise the points as clearly as possible.

- According to Michell (1997) Stevens (1951) avoided the problems of additivity by arguing that measurement implied isomorphism between what was being measured and the measurement system. Thus Stevens proposed various types of psychological scales, which have been adopted almost universally into psychology and which will be discussed later in this chapter.
- However, this raises a further difficulty. If measurement represents the empirical structure of what is being measured, it must first be necessary to show what that structure is. This is rarely done.
- As Michell (1997) points out, this further problem Stevens avoided by using an operational definition of measurement, in which what is measured is identified by the operations used to measure it. Thus intelligence is what is measured by an intelligence test.
- However, this argument is inconsistent with the scientific endeavour. Science takes the realist position that there is a real world, the object of knowledge which we seek to apprehend by the scientific method. Thus normally we would say that measuring X as longer than Z depended upon the fact that X was longer than Z. However, this is not so by Stevens' definition where all that X being longer than Z means is that it was so measured. Psychology, on this definition, consists of a study of the operations used in measurement, whereas a scientific psychology normally implies a realist view that there are psychological facts to be apprehended.

Conclusions

Michell (1997) somewhat controversially concluded that psychologists were deluded in imagining that their psychometric tests were scientific. Psychometric tests were, as has been shown, entirely different from those in the natural sciences and, in addition, no attempt was ever made to measure the empirical structure of the variables to be measured.

In Defence of Psychometrics

Ignoring for the moment the question of delusion, it is difficult to controvert the conclusions drawn by Michell. I accept the fact that psychometric measurement is different from measurement in the natural sciences and that strictly, therefore, it should not be called scientific.

However, in psychometrics there is now a vast body of research findings based upon the scores of tests and these scores have proved useful, as will be shown in later chapters both theoretically and in application. It would be absurd to jettison all this because the psychometric tests from which they were derived were different from the measures used in the natural sciences. To conclude this chapter, therefore, I want to look at the tests developed using the operational definitions of Stevens in more detail and to indicate, briefly, why they should not be abandoned.

Stevens (1946) argued that scales could be constructed such that a hierarchy of measurement, in terms of mathematical efficiency, could be constructed.

Ordinal Scales

In ordinal scales, as the name suggests, individuals are placed in rank order in respect of the attribute under measurement. In such scales there is obviously no indication of the absolute position of the subject on the variable and, an even greater difficulty, there is no indication of the distance between subjects. This implies that there is little quantitative information in ordinal scales. Indeed, to take the example of an intelligence test, an ordinal measure would fail to indicate how intelligent subjects were or the differences between them. Ordinal scales are far from scientific and should be avoided.

Interval Scales   *LACK OF TRUE ZERO*

Interval scales have three characteristics:

1   The rank order of subjects is revealed.
2   The distance between subjects is also indicated.
3   However, there is no information about absolute magnitudes of the variables.

The significance of these characteristics for the quality of measurement must now be scrutinised and I shall illustrate the problems and difficulties with reference to intelligence tests although, of course, they are pertinent to all psychological variables.

First, the lack of a true zero. All that can be done is to specify how far a subject's score deviates from the mean of a group. For example, a score 10 points above the average might be scored as +10 and a score 15 points below as −15 and so on. However, the significance of such a score depends entirely upon the group with which it is compared. Such comparisons are part of the process of test construction and development known as standardisation and this is discussed in Chapter 3.

This lack of true zero is inevitable with interval scales and this creates a further difficulty which is conceptual in nature. What would be the meaning of zero intelligence or zero extraversion, other than that the subject has died? This is exceedingly difficult to answer but the fact that this is the case implies that these variables are themselves unclear.

Although in interval scales distances between subjects are indicated, that is subjects are given scores, not simply ranked, it is only an assumption that the size of these intervals is equal all along the scale. Thus, on a test of intelligence, it is questionable whether a 10 point difference at the bottom of the IQ scale reflects the same difference in intelligence as it does in the middle and at the high end of the scale.

Nunnally (1978) argues that this assumption of equal intervals in interval scales is safe on the grounds that mathematical analyses of test scores from such interval scales leads to meaningful and replicable results, particularly in the field of abilities. Since such analyses depend on the equality of intervals, such clear results would be unlikely if these assumptions were unfounded. It must be pointed out that this is a critical issue in psychometrics since in both applied and theoretical applications complex multivariate statistical analyses are used, all depending on equality of intervals. Were it to be shown that this assumption was false, then not only would all psychometric findings be cast into doubt but future analyses would be restricted to the simple procedures which are permitted for ordinal scales. These problems of the applicability of statistical analyses will be discussed later.

Ratio Scales   *true zeros + equal intervals*

Ratio scales are regarded in the work of Stevens (1945) as the ideal scale and, as we have seen, the fundamental scales of the natural sciences are of this kind. In ratio scales both the rank order and the distance between individuals is known. However, in contrast with interval scales, in ratio scales the distance from a rational or true zero is known. This means that there are equal intervals in these scales. Thus, as can be seen from our discussion of ordinal and interval scales, ratio scales avoid their problems, having true zeros and equal intervals.

What Types of Scale are Psychometric Tests?

The vast majority of psychological tests measuring intelligence, ability, personality and motivation, that is those tests which are largely the subject of this Primer, are interval scales. On tests of this kind, subjects each receive a score based upon the number of items to which they have given the keyed response. The keyed response is the correct response in tests of intelligence and ability but the notion of correct makes no sense in personality and motivation tests. Here responses to items are keyed for a scale. An example will clarify this issue which it is essential to understand since it will occur throughout the book. Take, for example, the item: 'Do you often fear the future? Yes/No.' This is an item typical of those in tests of personality. It is intended, as is obvious, to measure anxiety. Hence the item is keyed 'Yes'. Clearly there is no correct answer to such a question. It is keyed 'Yes' because it is presumed that this response indicates an anxious individual. A subject's score on an anxiety scale will consist of the total of such keyed responses.

From this description it is clear that such scales must be interval scales. Thus there is no true zero. It would be hard to argue that because subjects failed to endorse any of the keyed responses to such a scale that their anxiety scores were really zero. It is conceivable that with other items they might have obtained a low score. Incidentally, notice the low. One hopes that with a good test other items would not have led to a high score for obvious reasons.

The subjects' scores place them in order, as with ordinal scales, but also give distances (differences between scores) between them. However, it is an assumption, as has been argued above, that these distances are equal. In the main therefore, as this example shows, psychometric tests constructed from numbers of items are interval scales.

As Michell (1997) argued, and as was fully scrutinised earlier in this chapter, such tests are quite different from measures in the natural sciences. They are not ratio scales, and thus there are no true zeros. Furthermore, there are no units of measurement. What is added up in tests are responses to items but these are not units in the sense of that term in the natural sciences.

As we have discussed above, although it is only an assumption that the intervals of interval scales are equal it is an important, not to say critical assumption for psychometrics, since the findings in this field of psychology are based upon complex multivariate statistical analyses which depend upon equality of intervals. Indeed psychometrics as a quantitative science would be brought to a standstill without such analyses. The reasons for this must now be examined.

Types of Scale and what is Permitted Mathematically

This is necessarily a mathematical issue and one which is beyond the scope of this Primer. However, the arguments are not at all contentious and can be summarised without algebraic complexity. My summary owes much to the clarity of exposition in Nunnally (1978) and for more details readers should consult this excellent text or its more recent version (Nunnally and Bernstein, 1994).

Ratio scales are open to the fundamental operations of algebra and arithmetic: addition, subtraction, multiplication and division. This means that, as in the natural sciences, powerful statistical and mathematical methodologies can be applied to scales of this type. With interval scales, on the other hand, this is not true although addition and subtraction are permissible. An example will clarify this point. If one subject has forty items correct in an intelligence test, and another only five items, it is not meaningful to argue that the former is eight times more intelligent than the latter. Thus division and multiplication of scale values are dubious in meaning, although these calculations are possible for intervals. Ordinal scales, to complete this aspect of the discussion, are not open to any of these fundamental algebraic operations, which is why they should be eschewed by all serious psychometrists.

The critical issue of what algebra is possible with these different kinds of scale is a function of scale invariance and must be briefly discussed.

Scale Invariance

Ratio scales remain invariant if each score is multiplied by a constant. It is on account of this that it makes no difference whether we measure length in metres or yards. There are no changes in the rank order of points, the ratio of points or the zero point of the scales. As Nunnally (1976) argues, such scale invariance is a proof that a scale is a ratio scale.

Interval scales remain invariant if each score is multiplied by a constant and a further constant is added. This necessary addition of the constant does not alter the order of points in the scales nor the equality of intervals. However, it does change the ratio among scale points. Thus multiplication and division are permissible only for intervals in interval scales and not scale points.

On these grounds Nunnally (1976) claims that it is not improper to subject interval scales to mathematical and statistical procedures. This, of course, assumes that the intervals of such scales are equal, which in the case of psychological tests, as we have shown, is an assumption. However, the justification for this, it is argued, lies in the coherence of psychometric findings and their utility in application, the subject matter, indeed, of subsequent chapters of the Primer.

Conclusion of the Defence of Current Psychometrics

As has been pointed out, most psychometrists and psychologists accept as valid the current methods of psychometrics which yield interval scales with assumed equal intervals. The arguments for this acceptance are largely pragmatic and can be summarised below.

- The coherence of the findings. From psychometrics, a number of variables have been isolated in personality and psychology which make good psychological sense and which have proved useful in the development of psychological theory, particularly in the field of ability. All these findings are discussed in Chapters 5 and 6.
- Biometric studies of psychometric tests. Biometric studies of psychometric tests, investigating to what extent genetic factors account for their variance, indicate a considerable genetic determination. This implies that these tests are measuring something of fundamental importance, more than just the scores on a particular set of items. This work is also fully discussed in Chapter 5 and 6.
- Applied findings. As is scrutinised in Chapter 8 of this Primer, psychometric tests are applied in the occupational, clinical and educational settings. Again they have proved extremely useful, particularly in selection. There can be no doubt that the best method of selection for most jobs involves the application of psychometric tests, especially intelligence tests (Cook, 1998).
- Conclusions. All this has been sufficient to persuade psychologists that psychometrics, even if it differs from measurement in the natural sciences, is powerful in psychology. Any such differences, it is argued, are attributable to the indubitable fact that the subject matter of psychology differs from that of the natural sciences and, as a result, less perfect, but still effective methods are required.

Scientific Measurement: Conclusions

I accept these arguments in defence of current psychometrics. There is a considerable corpus of psychological knowledge built up from psychometric testing which it would be ridiculous to abandon. Current psychometrics, furthermore, has developed highly effective techniques of measurement which do much to produce rigorous measurement and these will be described in Chapters 3 and 4.

On the other hand, the arguments of measurement theory, exemplified by Michell (1990, 1997), are powerful. Psychometrics is not like the measurement of the natural sciences. It undoubtedly suffers from the fact that there are no clear units of measurement which lead to imprecision, because there are no benchmark measures, and to doubts concerning what is measured.

Thus we are confronted with an apparent paradox: psychometric measurement works, yet psychometrics is not scientific. One solution, as Cliff (1992) has argued, and this is the common one, is to ignore the work of measurement theory on the pragmatic grounds that psychometrics works. The second solution, and one certainly implied by Michell, is to abandon psychometrics.

Both these approaches are ill considered. I argue in the Primer and elsewhere (Kline, 1998, 1999) that there are now two tasks for psychometrics. Current psychometric work should continue in the applied field, since it does work better than anything else. In this area there are many improvements to be made to tests and methods, as will become obvious throughout this book.

However, theoretical psychometric research must change. The challenge of Michell must be met. It must be accepted that psychometric measurement is not scientific and that scientific measures have to be developed, however difficult this appears to be. I believe that this is possible and how this task might be begun is discussed in Chapter 9. Only when this occurs should current psychometrics be abandoned.

3
The Characteristics of Good Psychometric Tests

Introduction

So far in this Primer we have seen that psychometric testing has two related aims: the development of psychology as a science, by the provision of precise measurement, and the subsequent use of these measures in applied psychology, especially the fields of occupational, educational and applied psychology. In Chapter 2 it was pointed out that psychometric tests appeared to be quite different from the measures used in the natural sciences and that there was, therefore, some difficulty in regarding psychometrics as truly scientific. While these arguments, based on measurement theory, were difficult to refute it was pointed out that psychometric testing had yielded a corpus of results which were coherent and useful as a basis for psychological theory. In addition psychometric testing has proved valuable in the applied field. It was concluded, therefore, that research should attempt to develop psychometric tests which were genuinely scientific but that until this was done efficient psychometrics should not be abandoned.

The word 'efficient' in the previous paragraph should be noted. It is a matter of fact that many psychometric tests are technically poor, that is they certainly do not measure what they claim to measure and are essentially worthless for any purpose. On the other hand, a relatively small number of tests are highly efficient. Although different from the measures in the natural sciences, they measure with some degree of precision. The characteristics of such tests will be described below. Only tests which possess these characteristics are worthy of consideration, not only to use but in the scrutiny of research reports. Results from technically poor psychometric tests should simply be abandoned. Thus it is essential that what characterises good psychometric tests is fully understood.

The Characteristics of Good Psychometric Tests

A good psychological test has high reliability, high validity and high discriminatory power. In addition it possesses extensive norms. These four aspects of psychometric testing will be described and discussed in the following sections of this chapter. In addition to this the measurement model underlying psychometric tests will be explicated, necessary since some indices of reliability are derived from it. Before this is done, however, I shall explain a few elementary statistical terms which must be understood.

Some Important Statistical Terms

The Mean

This is the average of a group of scores. It is computed by summing the set of scores and dividing by the number of subjects who took the test. This formula may be found in the Glossary. The mean is a useful statistic to summarise the performance of a group on a test. For example, the mean score of ten-year-old children on an intelligence test would be higher than that of children a year younger. However, it is to be noted that this would not apply to all the children: some nine-year-olds would score more highly than some in the older group. Thus on its own the mean is not sufficiently accurately to describe group performance, on account of such variation.

Variance

Variance is a term describing the variations within a set of scores. If a test were administered and every subject scored the same score the variance would be zero. Variance is measured in terms of the deviations of each score from the mean. In the formula for the variance which is to be found in the Glossary it is to be noted that each deviation from the mean is squared. This is done in order to give more weight to the extreme scores. If the mean score on a test were 10, then a score of 12 represents a deviation of +2, a score of 6, −4 and so on. Actually the larger the variance the better the test since psychometrics is concerned with the study of individual differences.

The Standard Deviation

This, as the formula in the Glossary makes clear, is the square root of the variance. The standard deviation, like the variance, simply reflects the amount of variation in the set of scores. Groups are normally described in terms of their means and standard deviations. An example will clarify the issue. Suppose we have two tests each with a mean of 50. Test one has a standard deviation of 5 while test 2 has a standard deviation of 20. If a subject scores 55 on both tests the performance on test 1 is far superior to the performance on test 2. This is because on test 1, 55 is a full standard deviation away from the mean, whereas on test 2 it is only 1/4 of a standard deviation away from the mean. This example demonstrates that to compare two scores one must know not only the mean but the standard deviation. For this reason standard scores have been developed. Standard scores are always comparable. These are explained below and are fully discussed in a later section of this chapter.

Standard Scores

The formula for standard scores may be found in the Glossary. The standard score (z score) is the deviation from the mean divided by the standard deviation of the test. As was indicated, a score of 55 on both tests represented a better performance on test 1 than on test 2. This is made clear if we convert the two test scores to z scores. On test 1 the z score is 55–50 (the deviation)/5 the standard deviation. This yields a z score of 1. However, on test 2 the score is 5/20 which is .25. Thus z scores are always comparable because they take into account both the means and the standard deviations of the scores. Finally it should be noted that z scores are often transformed into other scales with more normal means. This is because for non-psychologists (and for many psychologists, who should know better) z scores with means of 0 and running from approximately +3 to –3, are hard to interpret. These simple transformations will be discussed in our section on standardising the test.

The Correlation Coefficient

Because the correlation coefficient is the basis of so much statistical analysis in psychometrics, it is essential to understand what it is. The formula for the correlation coefficient, for which the symbol is r, can be found in the Glossary. Correlation coefficients run from 1 through 0 to –1. They indicate the degree of agreement between two sets of scores (hence its use in measuring test–retest reliability, as will be seen). A correlation of +1 indicates perfect agreement while –1 indicates the opposite, that is the orders were completely reversed on the second test. A correlation of .0 indicates that there is no more agreement between the scores than could be expected by chance. An indication of how much agreement there is between sets of scores may be obtained by squaring the correlation coefficient. Thus a correlation of .8 indicates 64% agreement.

Now that these statistical terms have been explicated, we are now ready to scrutinise and discuss the four characteristics of good tests which were mentioned earlier in this chapter. I shall begin with reliability.

Reliability

Meaning   The reliability of a test has two meanings. One refers to the stability of the test scores over time. This is known as *test–retest reliability*. The other is concerned with the internal consistency of the test and is called *internal consistency reliability*. I shall discuss each type of reliability separately.

Test–Retest Reliability

A good test has high test–retest reliability. It is one of the criteria by which a psychometric test is considered to be good or efficient. However, as is obvious, all turns on what is meant by high and this involves a discussion of how test–retest reliability is measured.

The Measurement of Test–Retest Reliability

Test–retest reliability is measured by administering the test to the same group of subjects on two occasions. The two sets of scores are then correlated. The minimum acceptable correlation for test–retest reliability is .7. This is for individual use. If a test is to be used simply with groups, for research purposes, a lower correlation coefficient might be tolerated but, as we shall see, the lower the correlation the larger the error in the scores. As is clear from our discussion of the meaning of the correlation coefficient this minimum figure for test–retest reliability of .7 indicates a modest agreement of just under 50%. However, it must be stressed this is a minimum.

Importance of Test–Retest Reliability

It is obvious that if anything is measured on two occasions, provided there are no changes, the measurements should be the same. Thus with precise measurement test–retest reliability ought to be perfect, that is a correlation of 1. In practice this is never the case with psychometric testing although in the case of ability and intelligence tests, test–retest reliability can be in the order of .9. The reasons for this are set out below.

Why Test–Retest Reliability is not Perfect

Real changes may have occurred   In assessing test–retest reliability the gap between retesting needs to be known. If, for example, we gave a short test of ten items and then retested immediately afterwards, most subjects would have identical sets of scores and the resulting reliability would be very close to 1. This, however, is an artefact of the procedure. Normally to establish the test–retest reliability of a test, there should be a gap of at least three months. However, in this time there may have been real changes on the variable which affected the scores of some individuals. If retesting children, for example, one must be aware that sometimes progress is not steady but occurs in sudden improvements. This saltatory progress clearly diminishes test–retest reliability.

Other factors producing changes   There are other factors which can distort scores at any one time of testing: feeling ill; being very tired; feeling anxious about some recent event; anxiety about the test which is obviously less on the second or subsequent testing; in a long test fatigue or boredom affecting the latter part; turning over two pages at once; breaking one's pencil; being distracted by an uncomfortable seat or a hot room. Clearly all these factors will affect the performance on psychometric tests and thus tend to reduce test–retest reliability and this is not intended to be a complete list. These are generally subsumed under test error.

Test error   This problem will be discussed in more detail later in this chapter. Here it is sufficient to note that it is generally agreed that psychometric tests, even the best, measure the intended variable together with a certain amount of error. Thus the variance in test scores is in part attributable to error variance. This accounts for imperfect test reliability. Indeed, as shall be seen, test reliability is used as an index of test error. The lower the reliability, the higher the error.

Test error, change and test–retest reliability   It is sometimes argued that the demand by psychometrists for high test–retest reliability must be mistaken because since psychological variables change such high reliability must be misleading. This argument, however, is confused. It is only when a test has high retest reliabilty that small changes can be detected at all. I shall exemplify this from the measurement of length. Suppose we had a ruler with very poor test–retest reliability. For a line of 10 feet it might give, on each measurement, a variety of lengths perhaps ranging from 9 to 12 feet. In this instance a change of 6 inches could never be detected. The confusion springs from the fact that the measurement of test–retest reliability assumes that the variable (intelligence, for example) has not changed and that the imperfect correlation is due to error. If we have reason to think that the variable has changed it would be absurd to attempt to measure test–retest reliability. Cattell (1957) refers to real changes as function fluctuation and this is quite different from test error. Certainly if we attempt to measure a variable such as anger which obviously does change over time, an index of test–retest reliability is not appropriate.

Conclusions Concerning Test–Retest Reliability

It is obvious that, except in certain specialised instances, test–retest reliability should be as high as possible.

Internal Consistency Reliability

Meaning of Internal Consistency Reliability

The majority of psychometric tests consist of a number of items. The score obtained by a subject depends on the number of items which were correct or to which the keyed response was given. Thus the internal consistency reliability reflects the extent to which each item is measuring the same variable. An example will clarify this point. If we have a test of intelligence we should expect each item to be measuring intelligence and not some other ability such as verbal or spatial ability. The more this is the case the higher the internal consistency reliability of the test and the reliability coefficients to be expected of a good test are similar to those for test–retest reliability. All this is so obvious as to be banal. However, the fact is, especially with personality and motivation tests, that internal consistencies are often far below the criterion of .7 and this must cast doubt on what they measure. Scrutiny of books listing psychological tests demonstrates the surprisingly low internal consistencies of many tests, even well-known ones such as the MMPI-2 (Graham, 1990), as can be found in Kline (1999) or Cronbach (1994). This is a serious defect in a psychometric test and such tests should not be used unless, despite this low reliability, there is clear evidence of validity, a valid test being one that measures what it claims to measure.

Measurement of Internal Consistency Reliability

The standard measure of the internal consistency of a test is the alpha coefficient, which is interpreted as if it were a correlation. It represents the correlation of the items in a test with any other set of items measuring the same variable, and the formula for coefficient alpha is to be found in the Glossary. The rationale of the alpha coefficient is complex but it will be explicated in a later section of this chapter on the theory of test error. There are more simple ways of measuring internal consistency which approximate alpha and clearly indicate the nature of this form of reliability. In the split-half method, for example, the odd-numbered items are correlated with the even, or the first 20 items with the last 20, which works well with a personality test but not a test of ability where the items get harder as the test continues.

Reliability and Test Length

It can be shown (for example, Nunnally, 1978) that reliability increases with the number of items. This increases until the test is so long that boredom and fatigue begin to affect responses. Ten items are usually considered the minimum number for a reliable test.

Importance of Internal Consistency

Internal consistency reliability is important for a number of reasons which I shall set out below, some briefly since they have been mentioned in the previous section.

- A test cannot correlate with anything more highly than it does to itself. This is important because the validity of a test and often its utility depends on its correlations with other criteria. For example, we would expect a test of intelligence to correlate with success at academic work (provided this was not one of the social sciences), or success at complex problem solving. Poor internal consistency sets a limit to such prediction. There is a correction for this defect (correction for attenuation due to low reliability) and the formula can be found in the Glossary) but although this is used one must be cautious in interpreting such inflated correlations.
- As has been argued, it is a peculiar measuring instrument if different parts of it are measuring different variables, as must be the case with low reliability.
- As will be discussed later in this chapter, low internal consistency implies considerable error of measurement.

Conclusions Concerning Internal Consistency Reliability

For all these reasons the majority of psychometrists regard internal consistency reliability as essential for a good test. However, Cattell (1957), certainly one of the most distinguished psychometrists, has always argued against this conventional position.

Can a test be too internally consistent? The Cattellian argument is remarkably simple. If a test is highly internally consistent it is likely to be somewhat narrow and specific in its item content. Thus, for example, in personality tests if we paraphrase items internal consistency is bound to be high. In a test of extraversion many items about liking lively parties will raise internal consistency but at the expense of covering other aspects of the variable. This is particularly important in short tests. If a test is short and internally consistent it is almost inevitably what Cattell (1957) calls a bloated specific. It is unlikely to be valid.

Actually there is a statistical basis for such low validity. If each item in a test is regarded as a predictor of the test score it follows that we will get maximum prediction from all the test items if each item correlates with total test score but has a zero correlation with other items. This is so because if, for example, one item were perfectly correlated with another item, it contains no extra information and is entirely redundant. This means that high internal consistency must be antithetical to validity.

This argument by Cattell is hard to refute. Consequently it is reasonable to expect high internal consistency reliability for a test, say around .8, but to be cautious of extremely high values, especially with short tests. Inspection of the items will reveal in most cases whether or not the test is too specific.

Final Conclusions Concerning Reliability

Test–retest reliability should be as high as possible. It is clearly absurd if a test gives different scores on different administrations. Internal consistency reliability should also be high but in the case of short tests high reliability may mean that the test is too narrow in item content. Finally it must be noted that while high reliability is necessary for test validity it is not sufficient. A test can be reliable but not valid. We must now turn, therefore, to the subject of test validity.

Validity

Meaning

A test is said to be valid if it measures what it claims to measure. Although this definition sounds banal, it is important because critical scrutiny of tests, far too rare even among psychometricians, reveals that the vast majority of psychological tests are far from valid (see, for example, Cattell and Johnson, 1986, Cronbach, 1994 and Kline, 1999). It is by no means obvious what a test measures from a simple inspection of its items, for reasons which will become clear in our discussion of validity.

Measurement of Validity

The measurement, or perhaps more properly, the assessment of validity is a far less precise and more subjective procedure than is the case for reliability. There is no single numerical index of test validity. Rather there are a number of different approaches to establishing the validity of a test and these are set out below.

Face Validity

Face validity refers to the appearance of a test. A test is said to be face valid if it appears to measure what it claims to measure. However, unfortunately, face validity bears no necessary relationship to true validity. It is a good rule to assume that the validity of a test cannot be gauged from the item content, especially with personality and motivation tests and other similar questionnaires. With tests of ability and attainment, face validity can be a rough guide but it is only rough since it can be shown that many such test items measure mainly *g*, or general ability (for example, Kline, 1991). If we take a typical personality test item such as 'I am quite easily frightened' to which subjects have to respond 'Yes' or 'No' there are several reasons why the validity of this item as a measure of anxiety might be dubious. First, there is a problem with the meaning of the item in that 'quite easily' will be differentially interpreted by different people. This is because we simply do not know how easily others are frightened and hence two people with very different thresholds of fright could claim that they were easily frightened. This alone renders the item dubious. Then there are problems of genuine delusion in which quite timid people think that they are bold and vice versa. Furthermore, especially in selection, there is deliberate distortion. In a selection procedure for a job requiring boldness, who would endorse the item positively? Finally it has been shown that questionnaire items are subject to response sets (discussed fully in Chapter 6) of which the two most important are social desirability, the tendency to put the response which is the most socially desirable, and acquiescence, the tendency to respond 'Yes' to an item regardless of content. In brief, face validity is not a good guide to true validity. Its only value is to make psychometric tests appear reasonable to subjects and this goes some way to ensure their cooperation.

Concurrent Validity

The measurement of the concurrent validity of a test entails the correlation of that test with other tests in one administration, hence the name. Obviously this requires that there is some benchmark measure of the variable if the correlation is to be meaningful. For example, if we are trying to establish the validity of a new intelligence test we might correlate it with a benchmark measure of intelligence. A high correlation would be a demonstration of concurrent validity. This example raises several problems with the notion of concurrent validity which are set out below.

Benchmark measures   In our discussion of scientific measurement in Chapter 2 it was pointed out that fundamental measures in the natural sciences all had units of measurement which had benchmarks for accuracy, for example the kilogram held in Sevres. However, the notion of benchmark measures in psychometrics is different. Here it refers not to units of measurement but to actual tests which are regarded as excellent measures of their variables. In fact in psychology, as I have pointed out (Kline, 1998), there are very few such tests although, in respect of intelligence, the Wechsler Scales (Wechsler, 1958) are so regarded and for extraversion and the anxiety factor, in the field of personality, the EPQ (Eysenck and Eysenck, 1975) is of benchmark quality. Thus the majority of psychological variables have no such benchmark measures and this raises an obvious difficulty for establishing concurrent validity.

Concurrent validity where there are benchmark measures   Even if there is a benchmark measure there are difficulties with the notion of concurrent validity. The most obvious one is that if there is such a benchmark measure there must be little need for a new test. This is correct and in such cases the new test being validated must be entirely different or fulfil some practical need. For example, the Wechsler Scales (Wechsler, 1958) cannot be administered to groups but are individual tests, which need considerable training to use. Thus a brief five-minute intelligence test which correlated highly with these scales would be excellent. However, the benchmark EPQ is a simple, easy to administer questionnaire and the value of producing another similar inventory is dubious. In brief, with benchmark measures the new test must be radically different in some important features. Sometimes, concurrent validity for a test is shown by correlating the test with others of a similar name even though the evidence for the validity of these is attested by the same circular procedures. Self-esteem tests, as I have demonstrated (Kline, 1999), exemplify the dangers of such circularity in concurrent validity.

Concurrent validity where there are no benchmark measures   This, of course, is the normal case when we are trying to establish the validity of a test. Here, all that can be expected is a modest positive correlation of about .3 to .5. Any higher than this and our test would be too similar to the non-benchmark measure. This is clearly unsatisfactory since modest correlations of this kind are open to many different interpretations. For example, I developed a test, purportedly measuring the anal character (Freud, 1908). There were no acceptable measures of this syndrome so all that could be done was to correlate the scale, AI3Q (Kline, 1971), with measures of similar but not identical psychological variables, with the hope of demonstrating the modest but positive correlations discussed above. Such an approach to concurrent validity actually might be labelled construct validity, which I shall discuss later in this section. Clearly, with no benchmark measures, the demonstration of concurrent validity is highly subjective and somewhat unconvincing.

Predictive Validity

A test is said to have predictive validity if it is able to predict some appropriate criterion. A typical example concerns intelligence tests. Thus the validity of such tests is attested by the fact that they can predict academic performance both in school-leaving examinations and at university, even when they are administered at the age of five, as in the studies of gifted children by Terman and Oden (1959) or at the age of eleven, as is fully documented by Vernon (1961). Indeed, as Jensen (1980) has shown, intelligence tests are the best predictors of learning ability and they are, in addition, the best single predictor of occupational success (Ghiselli, 1966 and Schmidt and Hunter, 1998). However, impressive as this is, two problems concerning predictive validity must always be borne in mind. The first concerns the size of the correlations.

The Size of the Correlations in Predictive Validity

The correlation between a test and most real-life criteria is likely to be far from unity since many different variables are likely to be linked to them. Even academic success which would appear to be clearly related to intelligence is affected by other factors: the skill of teachers, the peer group of the children, the family circumstances, and health of the child, and this is not a complete list. Thus a modest but positive correlation would be acceptable as evidence of predictive validity. Thus the question arises of what is a reasonable minimum. One approach, which is frequently adopted, is virtually delusional. This is to regard as support for predictive validity any correlation which is statistically significant. Since this is an error which intrudes into much of psychometrics I shall divert at this juncture to a brief discussion of the implications and meaning of statistical significance.

Diversion on the Meaning of Statistical Significance

Some statistical tests, for example, the *t* test to test the difference between mean scores, and the correlation, of relevance to this discussion, are said to be statistically significant or not. If we correlate two sets of scores we assume the null hypothesis which states that there is no correlation between the scores and that any departures from zero are due to chance. It is possible to compute, given the numbers in the sample, what the probability is of any given correlation arising by chance when the actual correlation is zero. If this probability is 5% or less the correlation is said to be significant, meaning that it is unlikely to be due to chance. This significance is referred to as the *p* value (*p* standing for probability). There are, therefore, various levels of significance. The .05 level means that there are 5 chances in 100 or less that such a value could have arisen by chance. The .01 level means that there is only one chance or less and so on. The smaller the level of probability, the greater the level of statistical significance and, consequently, the more confidence we can have that the correlation did not arrive by chance in that particular sample. All this sounds fine, but the notion of statistical significance is open to a number of misunderstandings, arising from two related issues.

1   The confusion of statistical significance with psychological significance. It may turn out that a personality test, for example, can predict job performance with a correlation of .20 and that this is significant. However, as was explained in our discussion of correlation, squaring the coefficient indicates the amount of common variance – in this case 4%. Thus our significant correlation predicts only 4% of the variance in job success. This is not impressive, which is obvious if we reverse the claim: 96% of the variance remains unexplained. Although statistically significant such a correlation has little psychological meaning.

2   Sample size and statistical significance. This confusion arises from the simple statistical artefact that statistical significance is linked to sample size for obvious reasons. With a sample of 2000 a correlation of .17 is significant. However, this indicates only a very slight agreement. On the other hand, with a small sample of 40 subjects a correlation of .38 is not significant. This is because with so small a sample a few outlying pairs of scores in agreement have a powerful influence on the size of the correlation coefficient.

Conclusions Concerning the Interpretation of Correlation Coefficients and their Magnitude in Studies of Predictive Validity

In effect we have to set a minimum size for regarding a correlation coefficient as being of any practical or psychological significance. This is usually set at .3 which accounts for just under 10% of the variance. This, needless to say, must have been derived from a sample large enough to render it significant. It makes good sense to regard the .01 level of significance as significant rather than the more lax 5% level. There are two other points which deserve notice before we end this diversion on the meaning of statistical significance. The first concerns the sample size. Samples need to be large enough to allow statistical significance. However, they must be representative of the population in which we are interested. If we are studying the factors influencing intelligence in boys a huge sample drawn from one school is not as valuable as a representative sample drawn from many schools even if this is smaller. The second concerns the arbitrary nature of significance levels. It is simply a rational decision to fix the minimum significance level as 5 chances in 100. It could have been 3, 8 or 10 or anything at all. To regard, therefore, the attainment of statistical significance as not some sort of holy grail but the actual thing, as some researchers appear to do, particularly in the social sciences, must be mistaken, as all our arguments make clear.

The Second Difficulty with Predictive Validity: Establishing a Criterion

In the case of intelligence tests, as has been shown, it is possible to establish meaningful criteria to investigate their predictive validity. Furthermore, that a test given at the age of 5 years can predict real-life performance so well is impressive support for the validity of a test, far more so than with concurrent validity which involves correlations with other tests. However, it is often the case with many psychological variables that to establish a meaningful and convincing criterion is difficult. Take, for example, extraversion and tough-mindedness, two of the personality factors which are generally agreed to account for considerable variance in the field of personality (Mathews and Deary, 1998). What could the predictive criteria for these variables be? It is possible to make tentative suggestions. Thus if we tested extraversion and tough-mindedness at the age of 18, we might look 10 years later at what jobs these subjects did. In the case of extraversion we might rate jobs for the involvement of the variable, for example, high for publicans and those dealing with the public and low for librarians. However, it would be absurd to expect any but very small correlations since there are so many factors other than personality which affect what job one has, and this raises great difficulties with interpreting the results, as has been discussed. In the case of tough-mindedness the problem becomes even more difficult and I can think of no convincing criteria for predictive validity.

Conclusions Concerning Predictive Validity

Where convincing and reliable criteria can be found, predictive validity is good evidence for the validity of a psychometric test. Often, however, the criteria necessarily imply modest or small correlations and this makes interpretation difficult and such evidence for validity is therefore equivocal.

Incremental and Differential Validity

These are two approaches to the demonstration of test validity which are used in applied psychology, particularly occupational psychology. A test is said to have incremental validity when in a battery of tests, perhaps in selection, it correlates (even only moderately) with the criterion, but zero with the other selection tests. In this case the correlation, although small, adds in new information and is thus valuable. The demonstration of such incremental validity requires the multiple regression of all the tests with the criterion score. Differential validity is a similar concept to that of differential validity. The most simple example is that of interest tests. These possess incremental validity for academic success because the scores have different correlations with different subjects, for example science or French. Vernon (1961) has a useful discussion of these two approaches to validity.

Content Validity

As the name suggests, the validity of the test is determined from the content of the items. This approach to validity is suited only to tests of attainment or ability where the items are designed to reflect some definite and specified skill or knowledge. For example, we might want our students to be able to name by ear the note B flat. Thus the musical test item in which this note was played and which required students to name it would have content validity. The content validity of a whole musical test could be ascertained by allowing experts to examine the items and if there were agreement that the item set covered important and pertinent aspects of musical ability, the test could be said to have content validity. Clearly the same procedures could be applied to any field where there was such definite and precise knowledge. Two points need to be noted concerning content validity.

1   Distinction between face validity and content validity. In an earlier section of this chapter we pointed out that face validity, the appearance of a test, was not a good guide to real validity. However, although both face validity and content validity involve item examination, there is a clear distinction between them. Thus there can be no dispute about what constitutes musical knowledge and thus whether an item tests such knowledge, and in fields where this is so, examination of the content reveals content validity. With most psychological variables, such as intelligence or spatial ability, and especially so in the case of motivation and personality tests, there is no such agreement. This being the case content validity is ruled out and item examination becomes simply a matter of face validity which is a poor guide to what a test actually measures.
2   Content validity and other forms of validity. Even where there is good agreement on the content validity of a test further evidence is needed of validity. This is because a set of items in any field of ability, despite the item content, may be so phrased that many of them test intelligence as well as the variable intended. As will be stressed throughout this Primer, it is essential that all tests are univariate, that is measure only one variable. A test which measures more than one variable cannot be accurately interpreted and identical scores may not be psychologically the same.

Construct Validity

It is clear from our discussion of the various types of validity that none is entirely satisfactory and applicable to all types of test. Thus face validity is not a guide to true validity, concurrent validity is applicable only where there are benchmark measures for the variables, and predictive validity, although powerful, is only effective where clear criteria can be established. Differential and incremental validity are only useful in the applied fields alongside other measures, and content validity, finally, is suited only to fields with clearly specified skills and knowledge. To obviate these problems as far as is possible, Cronbach and Meehl (1955) developed an approach to test validation, a test known as construct validity.

Meaning of Construct Validity

In establishing the construct validity of a test the first step involves the definition and delineation of the meaning of the test variable. A construct, in the sense of construct validity, is essentially a concept. Hence delineating the meaning of the test variable means clarifying the nature of the concept to be measured. From this we can draw up hypotheses concerning the test scores which can then be investigated. If these are rejected the test has poor construct validity. However, if they are not rejected but supported by the findings the test can be said to have construct validity.

An Example of Construct Validity

If we wished to establish the construct validity of a new test of anxiety, we would set up the following hypotheses based upon our knowledge of the construct of anxiety. These hypotheses, it should be noted, effectively comprise the two main approaches to validity which we have already described – predictive and concurrent validity – together with studies which are unique to construct validity.

1 The anxiety test should correlate positively and substantially (>.4) with other tests of anxiety (concurrent validity).
2 The test should not correlate with other personality tests considered not to measure anxiety.
3 The test should not correlate with tests of ability since these are considered to be independent of personality (Cattell, 1957, for example).
4 High scorers on the anxiety test should within a given period of time (say two years), compared with low scorers (the groups being matched on other variables), show more indications of psychiatric disturbance – visits to out-patient clinics, more antidepressants and so on. This is an example of predictive validity.
5 Those above the norm for anxiety but not the highest scorers should show improved academic performance compared with controls. This is a common finding in studies of academic performance and personality (see Braden, 1995).

Discussion of these Hypotheses

These five hypotheses are typical of those used in construct validity. It is obvious that if all were confirmed it would be difficult to dispute that the test was a measure of anxiety. This is because each hypothesis was derived from an analysis of the psychological meaning of the term. Even if the face validity of the test were poor any test whose scores fitted the set of hypotheses must be a test of anxiety, by virtue of the nature of the variable. That is why most test constructors, particularly of personality and motivation tests where straightforward tests of predictive validity are difficult to set up, agree with Cronbach and Meehl (1955) that construct validity is the best approach to validating a test. However, there are two difficulties with construct validity which our example illustrates. This concerns the subjective nature of the evidence and the equivocal conclusions which can arise from the results of the studies. First, it is always possible to argue that hypotheses are or are not pertinent to the validity of the test. Although our example was clear, it was chosen for that reason. Often considerable ingenuity is required to formulate the relevant hypotheses. To that extent there is undoubtedly a subjective element in construct validity. There is equivocation too. It is usually the case that not all the hypotheses are confirmed. Thus if only a majority are supported although the validity of the test may be regarded as confirmed, as argued, the results are not unequivocal.

Conclusions Concerning Validity

From this discussion it is clear that the validity of a test is not clear-cut, as was the case with reliability. There is no one single validity coefficient. Construct validity is the best approach where a mosaic of results is considered in total. What is clear, however, from the discussion, is the plain fact that the demonstration that a test is valid is not a simple matter, and, as will be apparent throughout this book, many tests lack good evidence that they are valid.

Discriminatory Power

This is the third characteristic of good psychometric tests and it can be dealt with briefly. The meaning of discriminatory power can be easily illustrated. If we were required to judge the quality of essays it would not be difficult (although the judgements might well be wrong) to put them into three groups: excellent, average and poor. However, these judgements have low discriminatory power since only three groups were created and in all likelihood the average group would be the largest. Vernon (1961) showed that nine categories are about the most that can be used with any degree of reliability or validity in any kind of rating procedure.

Thus the more discriminations a test can make, the more discriminatory it is. Suppose we have a test of 30 items. The maximum possible discrimination it could make would be if at each score, 0 to 30, there were an equal number of subjects. This would be perfect discrimination. If a frequency distribution of these scores were drawn it would be a straight horizontal line. The worst discrimination possible would be if every subject obtained the same score, for example 10. This would be no discrimination at all. Of course such extremes are virtually impossible to obtain with real data on real tests but it is obvious from this example that tests must vary in their discriminatory power.

In the study of individual differences the greater the discriminatory power of a test the better and for this reason Ferguson (1949) developed an index of discriminatory power, delta, of which the formula may be found in the Glossary. Delta runs from 1 to 0, 1 being perfect discrimination, 0 being the worst case. A normal distribution has a discriminatory power of .93 and in general tests ought to have deltas greater than .9.

Such then are the characteristics of good psychometric tests: high reliability, validity and discriminatory power. We shall now turn to a fourth important quality of good tests, the possession of good norms, although unlike the others this is not intrinsic to the test, as shall be seen.

Standardising the Test

Norms are sets of scores from specified groups of subjects and standardising a test involves obtaining scores from relevant groups. Thus on a test of anxiety we should need norms for the general population and norms for different neurotic groups such as depressives or hysterics.

Necessity for Norms

In Chapter 2 we showed how psychological tests differed from those in the natural sciences because they lacked a true zero. This made norms essential for interpreting the meaning of a test score, although it should be pointed out that even for true ratio measures such as length norms are useful (but not essential), as in studying the development of height in children. A score of 6 on a test is simply not meaningful without either a zero or norms.

Sampling in Setting up Norms

Almost all psychometric tests possess norms but many of these are based on samples so small or so unrepresentative as to be misleading. It is essential that a sample reflects the population it is intended to represent. An example will clarify this point. The proportions of males, females, social classes, types of education and other similar parameters in the population should be found in the sample. This means that for a sample of the general population, the sample size should be large, certainly several thousand, although this will vary depending on the sampling method. It is not only essential that the proportions of each group are accurately represented in the sample but the numbers in each group should be large enough to represent it – hence the need for large samples.

Sampling Methods

There are two sampling methods: random sampling and stratified sampling. In random sampling we ensure, as the name suggests, that no bias can enter into the selection of the sample by random selection. If the whole population is listed then a computer can generate random numbers to select a sample from it, or every nth person can be selected, the size of n being set such that a large enough sample will be selected. Stratified sampling, on the other hand, demands that the main strata of the population, social class, education, sex, etc., be established and a sample built up to represent this. The strata chosen will be those most relevant to the test variable and the population. For example, in a tribal society all the tribes need to be sampled. In each group 300 is regarded as a minimal sample size so with a large number of strata, the sample soon becomes huge. Examination of the norms for many tests shows that that they fail to meet these criteria.

Specialised Norms

For some tests more specialised norms are often of more value than a huge general sample. For example, in a test to be used in job selection, norms showing the scores for various occupations would be highly useful. Similarly in a test for use in clinical psychology norms for various clinical groups would be appropriate. Here the numbers need not be so large as is the case for the general population, but they must be representative and of a size sufficient to minimise statistical error (100 subjects is a minimum). Thus, for example, a sample of electrical engineers should be drawn from a representative sample of companies which employ them rather than just one or two large employers.

Types of Norm

Norms are intended to enable the test user to see where any particular score stands relative to the normative group. Thus essentially what is required is a distribution of scores. Norms take many forms and here I shall describe the most widely used varieties.

Percentiles

A percentile is defined as the score below which a given proportion of the normative groups falls. Thus a subject at the 98% percentile is clearly a very high scorer. Percentiles are simple to understand and for this reason are useful in applied psychology for explaining the meaning of test scores. However, they have two disadvantages. They are only ordinal in nature which makes them unsuited to statistical analysis (see Chapter 2). In addition they distort the distribution of scores. Thus they exaggerate small differences around the mean score and compress differences at the extremes of the distribution.

Standard Scores

Standard scores are transformations of raw or obtained scores such that any given standard score is always equivalent. There are different forms of such standard scores but each is easily computed from the basic standard or z score which was described in an earlier section of this chapter. To refresh the reader's memory, a z score is computed by dividing the deviation of a score from the mean by the standard deviation, all terms previously described. However, such scores have a mean of zero and run from approximately –3 to +3. Not only are z scores comparable, it is also apparent how far each score deviates from the mean, which is not the case with raw scores. However, the narrowness of the scale is awkward and these z scores can be easily transformed into more familiar scales.

Standard Scores with Means of 50 and Standard Deviations of 10

This is by far the most common transformation of scores. A z score of 0 = 50, 1 = 60 and 1.5 = 65, for example. The formula for such transformations may be found in the Glossary. Transformations of z scores can utilise any mean and any standard deviation. Transformed scores are always comparable, as was the case with z scores, to scores with the same mean and standard deviation.

T scores

These are standard scores with means of 50 and standard deviations of 10 which have been normalised, that is their distribution has been made to follow that of the normal curve (see Glossary). T scores should only be used where the distribution of raw scores was approximately normal or where there is some theoretical reason to expect a normal distribution, as in the case of intelligence.

Miscellaneous Types of Norm

Cattell for many of his tests (for example, the 16PF test, a personality questionnaire) (Cattell et al., 1970) uses Stens. Stens are normalised standard scores with means of 5.5 and SDs of 2. Many intelligence tests use standard normalised scores with means of 100 (hence 100 is the average IQ) and SDs of 15, occasionally 16.

Summary and Conclusions Concerning Test Standardisation

It may be concluded that norms are essential for the interpretation of test scores. However, such norms must be derived from large and representative samples of the relevant populations. Percentiles are crude norms compared with standard scores. The most commonly used standard score is that with a mean of 50 and an SD of 10. Normalised scores such as *T* scores should only be used when there is good reason to expect such a distribution.

The Classical Model of Test Error

To complete this chapter outlining the characteristics of good psychometric tests I shall introduce the statistical model underlying test scores. Although a full mathematical treatment is beyond the scope of this Primer (for this readers are referred to Nunnally and Bernstein (1994) or Kline (1999) for a simplified account) an understanding of the basic concepts is useful for a better understanding of reliability and validity.

The Model

It is assumed that test scores, referred to as obtained or fallible scores, comprise two sources of variance: true score variance and error variance.

Error Variance

Error variance refers to variance attributable to random error not systematic error. All measurements are compounded to some extent by error, even scientific measurements although in these cases it is usually small and of little significance. Random error in psychometric tests is often considerable. The sources of random error are many: fatigue, emotional upsets, misreading the items, too few items, misunderstanding the instructions, poor testing conditions, for example.

True Score

The true score is a notional concept. It is the score a subject would obtain if all the possible items in the relevant universe of items were administered. Thus it is assumed that, for each variable, there is universe of items. It is further assumed that the items in a test are a random selection of such items.

Consequences of the True Score Model

There are important consequences of this model which are set out below.

The Obtained Scores

The obtained score on a test consists, therefore, of a mixture of true score and random error, according to the model. Thus the obtained score, on any occasion, differs from the true score on account of random error. However, if we were to retest a subject, on the same test, again and again, a distribution of scores would be obtained. It is assumed in the model that the distribution of such scores is normal (because random errors are hypothesised to be so distributed) and that the mean of this distribution approximates the true score. In practice such retesting is impossible and if it were done would introduce other problems of remembering the items and boredom. Thus in reality we make use of a single score or at most two scores as in test–retest reliability.

The Standard Error of Measurement

This is a critical statistic for any psychometric measurement and it is derived from the notion of the true score. Suppose that for any individual there is a large variance of obtained scores on a test. It follows from the true score model that there must be considerable error variance. The standard deviation (an index of variability which we have discussed) of such a distribution of obtained scores is itself an index of error. Thus if every obtained score for an individual were the same, the standard deviation would be 0, and there would be zero error. The larger this standard deviation the larger the error and since it is reasonable that the error is the same for all individuals this standard deviation of obtained scores or errors becomes the standard error of measurement. Of course we cannot test a subject so often that such a standard error of measurement can be obtained. Instead an estimate is computed from the test–retest reliability which involves two testings. It can be seen from our discussion that the higher the test–retest reliability is, the lower the test error. The formula for the standard error of measurement can be found in the Glossary. This also takes into account the variance of the test scores themselves.

Meaning and Importance of the Standard Error of Measurement (SEm)

As was pointed out above, the SEm is an estimate of the standard deviation of the distribution of obtained scores, which is assumed to be normal. Hence we can argue that, on the basis of the normal curve, given one obtained score for a subject, 68% of all scores would fall between the obtained score plus 1 SEm and –1 SEm, while 95% would fall between the obtained score and 2 SEms. In other words, the SEm sets confidence limits for an obtained score. This is important, as an example will show. If we have a test with an SEm of 5, and scores from two subjects of 10 and 6, we could not say that the former indicated a different performance from the latter, since both fall within 1 standard error of measurement. To be absolutely confident a difference should be greater than 2 SEms, that is 10 points. Since, as the formula indicates, the higher the test–retest reliability the less the SEm it is obvious why such reliability is considered so vital in psychometric testing.

Some other Consequences of the True Score Model

Nunnally (1978) and Kline (1999), especially the former author, develop the statistical consequences of the true score model of test variance in considerable detail. In this Primer I shall state the most important without the mathematical argument which can be found in these texts.

Internal Consistency Reliability is Essential

It can be shown that the correlation of an item with the true score equals the square root of its correlation with all the other items. This means that if test items correlate highly with each other they must be correlated with the true score.

Test Reliability Increases with the Number of Items

Since the true score is the score on the universe of items, the longer a test the greater its correlation with this total must be. Thus a long test of intercorrelating items is likely to measure the true score. It can be further shown that 10 items is about the minimum for a reliable test and that 30 items offers very high reliability (and thus measurement of the true score).

Coefficient Alpha

Cronbach (1951) developed what is regarded as the best method for estimating the reliability of a test. It can be shown that the square root of the alpha coefficient is an estimate of the correlation of the test score with the true score. The formula for coefficient alpha can be found in the Glossary.

Before concluding this chapter I want to issue a warning concerning the importance of the true score. In many texts statistical enthusiasm deludes common sense. The true score model is excellent for understanding psychometric test scores and for test constructors. However, all the deductions from the model which show incontrovertibly that the scores of reliable tests must be closely related to the true scores ignore one point. They assume that the true score of the items is the true score intended by the tester. Thus a reliable extraversion test may not measure extraversion because the items, although homogeneous, are not drawn from an extraversion pool but from a narrow pool about party-going or socialising, for example. This is an example of a bloated specific. Sometimes the items are spoiled by social desirability, that is the items are effectively about their political correctness. That accounts for my earlier claim that reliability is necessary but not sufficient validity. In other words despite the statistical links, it is always necessary to show what a reliable test measures.

Conclusions

In this chapter I have discussed the characteristics of good psychometric tests. I have shown that:

- Test–retest reliability is essential for a good test.
- Internal consistency reliability is also essential.
- Reliability on its own is not sufficient to ensure that a test is valid.
- Validity must be demonstrated not assumed and that for many tests construct validity is the best method for such a demonstration.
- Discriminatory power is important for a good test.
- Norms must be large and representative of the relevant populations.
- The classical theory of test error based upon the true score underpins all these claims and provides a standard error of measurement.

4
Test Construction

There is no doubt that even if psychometric tests differ from those in the natural sciences, as has been shown, those tests which possess the characteristics described in Chapter 3 are still good measures. However, not all psychometric tests are, in fact, reliable and far fewer are valid. However, if tests are properly constructed, reliability and validity can reach acceptable standards even with variables which are difficult to measure. In this chapter, therefore, the four most commonly used methods of test construction will be described and compared. When such methods are understood it will be easier to evaluate the quality of psychometric tests and, of course, to develop measures both for research and in the applied field.

The Item Pool

In my discussion of test construction, I shall assume that we have a pool or set of items from which we want to construct a test. I shall not say much about how such items are written or devised because this is the aspect of test construction which is not really the province of psychometrics. The content of items depends on what we want to measure and is thus part of the relevant branch of psychology. The psychometrist can construct, for example, a test of hysteria or achievement motivation, provided that he or she is given the items. The actual item writing has to be done by a specialist in those fields, although their form may be improved by the psychometrist.

Nevertheless, regardless of what a test purports to measure there are good and bad items, and some guidelines to writing items can be set out here. In fact this subject has proved endlessly fascinating for some psychometrists who have described item writing in considerable detail, see especially Angleitner and Wiggins (1988) for personality questionnaires and Kline (1986, 1999).

Items in Ability Tests

Items Must be Objectively Scored

This is essential for the reliability of the test. If items are subjectively scored differences arise between scorers and with the same scorer if the test has to be scored more than once. There are many types of objectively scorable items of which the most common is the *multiple choice item*. In this type of item five possible answers are given of which only one is correct. The other four choices, known as distractors, need to be selected such that they actually distract, that is some candidates choose each of them. Finally they should not be so alluring that high scorers select them rather than the correct response. Needless to say, there must be only one correct answer among the five choices. Other typical item types are true/false items which suffer from the fact that guessing has a 50% probability of success and matching items where two lists of unequal length have to be matched, for example authors and books. These last two items are often used in attainment tests.

The Item Content should Embrace the Relevant Field

If we are measuring verbal ability it is important that all aspects of verbal ability are covered. As mentioned above, if the field is more specialised, specialists should be asked to supply the items or should be consulted about the coverage of the field. Without full coverage the test is likely to be highly specific and not valid.

Personality Test Items and Items in Questionnaires

In the typical personality questionnaire or inventory subjects are asked questions about their behaviour, beliefs or feelings or they are given statements and they have to indicate whether these are true for them or not. Many are the pitfalls for the unwary in writing such items and set out below are a number of useful points or guidelines about such items.

Items must be Objectively Scorable

This has already been discussed in respect of ability tests and no more needs to be said except that all the types of item in personality questionnaires must fall into this category.

The Effects of Response Sets must be Minimised

In questionnaire items of all kinds two response sets – acquiescence and social desirability – can distort results. Acquiescence is defined as the tendency to agree with the item regardless of content. Social desirability reflects a tendency to endorse an item not reflecting its meaning but its social desirability. Thus, for example, impeccably politically correct readers of the *Guardian* could not be asked questions concerning sexual behaviour or morality without fear of such distortion. Guilford (1959) claims that both these response sets can be minimised by careful item writing. In the case of social desirability by thinking carefully about each item it is possible, to some extent at least, to predict what is likely to be socially desirable and not include it in items. In any case, as will be shown, socially desirable items can be easily discovered and eliminated in the process of test construction. Acquiescence is more of a problem. However, clear item writing about a specific behaviour rather than general tendencies goes some way to minimise it. For example, it is easier to put the acquiescent response to the item 'I enjoy sport', than it is to 'I play tennis once a week', if you don't. To avoid acquiescent scorers being confused with high scorers it is usual to have a test balanced in respect of items keyed 'Yes' and items keyed 'No'. Response sets have been fully discussed by Cronbach (1946) and Edwards (1957) has concentrated on the study of social desirability.

Item Forms

There are many different forms of questionnaire item and I shall discuss those most commonly used.

The dichotomous item   The most simple and one that works well, as evinced by the Eysenck Personality Questionnaire (Eysenck and Eysenck, 1975) which has unequivocal evidence of validity, is that which requires a response of 'Yes' or 'No'. If the items are statements a 'True'/'False' response format may be used which is equivalent. It might appear that the lack of a middle response indicating unsure or uncertain was a disadvantage since, obviously, there must many items for which for some subjects the dichotomous choice is unsatisfactory. However, tests have been tried with both formats and, in general, it can be said that the trichotomous version with an uncertain category is not so good (for example Bendig, 1959). This is because the middle category proves too attractive for some subjects and the resulting test scores, although positively correlated with the dichotomous form, show less evidence of validity.

The rating scale response format   Some questionnaires use rating scales as the response format. These can have 5, 7 or 9 points which indicate the extent to which the item applies to the subject completing the test. Depending on the wording of the items, these scales run from always to never or agree to disagree. For example: 'I have difficulty sleeping. Never, rarely, sometimes, frequently, always.' There are problems with these scales especially because few people use the extremes although there is also a small number who frequently use them. In addition the middle category can be appealing. The reason that some test constructors prefer this format is that, as will be discussed below, in the construction of tests, items need to be correlated. To some extent the accuracy of such correlations depends on the variance of the items and this increases with the length of the scales. This is an objection to the use of dichotomous items, in principle, although in practice many good tests are made up of such items. Attitude tests almost always use statements followed by 5-point rating scales indicating a subject's degree of agreement with the item. These are known eponymously as Likert scales (Likert, 1932). In summary, there is little to choose between rating scale response formats and the more simple dichotomous types. I prefer the latter just because they are more simple.

Forced choice items   Ipsative tests are characterised by the arrangements of their items into forced choices. Thus a test might be concerned to measure two variables, each represented by an item. Subjects are required to say which item they prefer. For example: 'going to the pictures with friends' (measuring extraversion) or 'making sure my records and books were properly ordered' (conscientiousness). There are two difficulties with ipsative tests:

1   Artefactual negative correlations. The point about ipsative tests which are made up of sets of such items is that the scores are bound to be arte-factually negatively correlated. This is simply because if you choose one item you cannot choose the other. Similar distortions occur when there are many variables. This means that the correlations between scores cannot be subjected to factor analysis, discussed later in this chapter, which has been one of the main statistical methods in elucidating the psychological meaning of psychometric test results.
2   Norms cannot be used. The scores subjects obtain are based upon rankings. However, rankings are not comparable between individuals. Thus, for example, subject A might rank Weetabix better than cornflakes although she disliked both and the former was only marginally preferable. The same ranking of subject B might reflect addiction to Weetabix which constituted the staple diet. Thus it is with the scores of ipsative tests which, therefore, are unsuited to norms. These arguments have been forcefully put by Cornwell and Dunlap (1994). For both these reasons ipsative tests are not recommended other than as a basis for discussion, a use of tests which is claimed to be valuable in career appraisal, but fails to utilise the numerical properties of the tests and seems somewhat wasteful.

Methods of Test Construction

In all the methods of test construction to be described below a pool of items is administered to subjects and subjected to some form of analysis with the aim of producing a valid and reliable test. It is essential in all these methods that adequate samples in terms of both numbers and representativeness are used. This means that to reduce statistical error 100 subjects are the absolute minimum but the larger the better. All analyses need replication on new samples, including separate samples for males and females.

Criterion-Keying

The principle of criterion-keyed test construction is simple. An item is selected from the pool if it will discriminate among the criterion groups.

Meaning of Criterion Group

Suppose that we wanted to screen out drug users, as is required in some military tasks. A criterion group of drug users could be set up together with controls, individuals of the same age, sex, education and social background. The two groups would be administered a pool of items and any item which could discriminate the groups would be selected for the final test. The selected items would be administered again to a new criterion group and controls, and all items which passed both trials would be selected for the final test. The best example of such a criterion-keyed test is the Minnesota Multiphasic Personality Inventory, the MMPI (Hathaway and McKinley, 1938). This test originally discriminated nine clinical groups but over the years more than 200 different scales were developed from the item pool (Dahlstrom and Walsh, 1960). Indeed this is the most widely used personality inventory in terms of published papers and it has recently been further devised and modernised as the MMPI-2 (Graham, 1990).

Problems with Criterion-Keyed Tests

Despite the considerable reputation of the MMPI, this method of test construction has some severe problems which make it difficult to recommend its use.

Difficulties with criterion groups   The establishment of meaningful and clear criterion groups is not simple. Thus with the MMPI the clinical groups used – hysterics and depressives, *inter alia*, – cannot be reliably classified. Thus the test does not discriminate so well in clinical groups classified by different criteria from those used in Minnesota, as is obvious. In addition, clinical diagnosis, even when the same criteria are used is not highly reliable (Beck, 1962). Furthermore this problem of the criterion group is not specific to clinical or psychiatric diagnosis. In industrial psychology the establishment of occupational groups is similarly problematic. For example, a group such as engineers or lawyers is extremely diverse. Thus the generalisability of the results from criterion-keyed tests is often dubious.

Meaning of criterion-keyed scales   There are problems concerning the psychological meaning of scales developed by criterion keying. This is easily illustrated by a scrutiny of the Strong Vocational Interest Blank (Strong, 1927) which purports to measure occupational interest and is a criterion-keyed test. An item was included in a scale if it discriminated members of one occupation from another, for example lawyers. The items in this test were entirely atheoretical. The only concern was whether they would discriminate. Thus a high score on the lawyer's scale means that the subject endorsed the items which discriminated lawyers. However, lawyers may differ from others on a considerable number of variables. Thus such a scale, even if the items are correlated, is not psychologically homogeneous and has no psychological meaning. This is not trivial since use of such scales, even if they work, provides no information about the nature of jobs or job success, which a meaningful scale would do.

Conclusions

In brief, criterion-keyed scales, being empty of psychological meaning, cannot be recommended unless all that is required is a quick screening when all other psychological information is irrelevant. Indeed, in fields where psychological theory is clearly important, as in clinical psychology, it can be argued that the use of such tests is a barrier to knowledge.

Item Analysis

The aim of item analysis is to produce from the pool of items a set of items which is homogeneous, that is internally consistent and univariate (measuring one variable). Such a test will then fit the classical model of test error, described in Chapter 3, in which it is assumed that a test score consists of true score (hence the demand that the scale be univariate) plus error, which is minimised by high internal consistency. That scales are univariate is important because if they are not two identical scores are not necessarily comparable. For example, a score of 10 on a univariate test means that the subject scored 10 on the underlying variable or factor. However, if the test measures 2 factors then the meaning is unknown: 5 + 5 or 4 + 6 and so on.

The Item-Analytic Method

The items are administered to a sample of subjects and two indices are computed: the correlation of the item with the total score *r* and the proportion putting the correct or keyed response (*p*). Items which meet the criteria on these two indices (see below) are then selected for a new test trial. All those passing the new trial form the final test provided that they reflect, in terms of content, all the aspects of the variable to be measured. The test must then be shown to be reliable, discriminating and valid.

Item-Total Correlation

The rationale for this index is simple. If we are constructing an intelligence test, then all the items ought to be measuring intelligence. If this is the case, then each item should correlate with the total score. If items fail to do so they must be measuring a different variable. These must, therefore, be rejected from the final test. It might be objected that if all the items in the pool were not measuring intelligence then this method is bound to fail. This is true. What the item-total correlation ensures is that the test is homogeneous, measuring one variable (but see below for further discussion of this point). That is why validity studies are required to show what this variable is. The criterion for inclusion is an item-total correlation of .3 or more.

The Proportion Putting the Keyed Response

The rationale for this criterion is also simple. If 100% put the same response to an item it might as well not be in the test for it has made no discriminations among the sample. This is true for all tests other than criterion-referenced tests where all that matters is that a subject gets the answer correct (see Chapter 3 on content validity). Thus items which fail to discriminate are usually abandoned. Items must have a *p* value of between 20% and 80%.

Item Content

Items are selected, as has been argued, if they meet these two criteria on *r* and *p*. However, it is essential that selected items also reflect the content of the item pool. If this is not so new items are written and tried out, although occasionally no items can be found that can be included in the test but this itself may be evidence that our original conception of the variable was wrong.

Variant of the Method

Coefficient alpha (see Chapter 3), a measure of the internal consistency of the test, can be computed for the whole set of items along with *p* and *r*. Then the item with the lowest *r* is removed and the alpha for the total is recomputed. This process continues item by item until alpha reaches its highest point. The total set of items remaining constitutes the selected items.

In practice this method produces a virtually identical test compared with the standard procedure.

Item Analysis and the Univariate Test

This item analytic method ensures that the test is homogeneous. But it does ensure that the test is univariate. If it so happened that the items in the item pool were measuring two correlated factors (say verbal ability and intelligence) then item analysis could select items which loaded both these factors. The resulting test, although homogeneous, would be a mixture of these two factors and for this reason would not be ideal. Note, however, that such a test might work in educational selection or even in job selection since both these factors are important for these criteria. So, practically, item analysis is a good method of test construction and the case of correlated factors is relatively uncommon. However, from the viewpoint of yielding precision measure, this is a problem.

Demonstrating the Reliability and Validity of the Test

After the items have been selected by item analysis and the results replicated with a new sample, it is necessary, as has been argued, to show that the test is valid and reliable.

Conclusions Concerning Item Analysis

Item analysis is a simple and effective method of test construction and many well-known tests have been developed using this approach. Jackson, for example, in the Personality Research Form (1974), has considerably developed and refined the method. It should be pointed out at this point that I have here indicated the principles of these methods of test construction rather than the exact procedures. Details of these can be found in Kline (1999), and in any case the analyses are always carried out by computer.

In brief, it can be argued that item analysis can yield good tests but that sometimes it can include items measuring different but correlated factors. For this reason, despite its greater statistical complexity, many test constructors employ factor analysis rather than item analysis, although with a clearly univariate set of items the results of item analysis and factor analysis are almost perfectly correlated (Barrett and Kline, 1982).

Factor Analysis in Test Construction

Before the use of factor analysis in test construction can be understood it will be necessary to describe factor analysis itself. This is a highly complex, statistical procedure with which many researchers, since the time of its first use by Spearman (1904), have regularly deluded themselves, as Nunnally (1978) argued. In the past such delusions were restricted to those who were acquainted with the algebra required for its computation. Now with the advent of high speed computing, there are no limits to the confusion created by factor analysis and this has led to some very unsatisfactory test construction and psychometrics. Below, without mathematical complexity, I shall set out the principles of factor analysis and define its terminology. I shall also set out some guidelines for reliable factor analyses. From this the proper use of factor analysis in test construction will become self-evident. It should also be mentioned that the psychometric findings on intelligence and personality, discussed in Chapters 5, 6 and 7, also depend on factor analysis, a technique critical to every aspect of psychometrics.

What is Factor Analysis?

Factor analysis is a statistical method for simplifying complex sets of data, usually correlation matrices (all the correlations between a set of variables, for example test items), and our discussion will be restricted to this type of analysis. If we correlate 100 test items the number of correlations between them is huge, 10 000, far more than anybody could look at and understand. Factor analysis gives a mathematical account of these correlations in terms of a few factors which can be understood. There is a simple test of a good factor analysis: from it we should be able to reproduce the original correlations. For example, if we are constructing a mathematics test we would hope to find that the correlations between the items could be accounted for by one huge factor and a number of small ones, so small that their influence could be discounted. The one large factor we would hope was mathematical ability. How this almost magical simplification comes about will be explicated later in this chapter but first the technical terms will be defined.

Factor

A factor is a construct or dimension which indicates the relationships between a set of variables. Royce (1967) has an even more precise definition: a factor is a construct operationally defined by its factor loadings. At its simplest a factor is a linear combination of variables.

Factor Loadings

A factor loading is the correlation of a variable with the factor. To construct a test (for example, mathematics) we factor analyse the correlations between the pool of items. After the computation we obtain a set of factors on each of which the items load. These factor loadings are the correlations of the items with the factors. Thus if we have a factor on which many of the items load we define it as mathematical ability – a dimension or construct which correlates with mathematical items. What else could it be?

Interpretation and Meaning of Factors

Table 4.1 shows an artificial example of a factor analysis which will clarify the meaning of factors and factor loadings as well as illustrate their interpretation. I shall suppose we have been constructing three personality scales: Extraversion, Neuroticism and Psychoticism, from a pool of items. I shall show loadings from 10 items. Items 1–3 are extraversion items, 4–6 neuroticism and 6–10 psychoticism.

Table 4.1 Factor loadings of 10 items from an item pool

Items	Factor 1	Factor 2	Factor 3	Factor 4
1	.42	.05	–12	.19
2	.65	.15	.21	.07
3	.48	.00	.18	.30
4	.02	.63	.22	.04
5	.31	.75	.13	.21
6	.19	.57	.04	.02
7	.00	.24	.66	.18
8	.03	.15	.45	.02
9	.17	.03	–62	.27
10	.09	.06	.11	.26

(handwritten annotations: "these load factor 1", "these factors good factor 2", "deny factor 3", "10 failed item", "doesn't load any factor")

Decimal points should be read before all figures in this table.

Interpreting the Factor Analysis in Table 4.1

If a factor is a construct defined by its factor loadings which are themselves the correlation of, in this example, the items with the factors, then the interpretation of Table 4.1 is relatively simple:

- Factor 1 is extraversion. The three extraversion items load this factor highly and they do not load other factors, except for item 3. This will be further discussed below.
- Factor 2 is neuroticism. Again the three neuroticism items load this factor and no other.
- Factor 3 is psychoticism. Three of the four psychoticism items load this factor. The fourth does not but this is an example of a failing item which does not load a factor and it would be rejected for the final test.
- Factors are defined by their loadings. As discussed above this example illustrates how factors are defined by their loadings. To compute the statistical significance of factors is not simple and it is usual and convenient to regard a loading of .3 or more as salient and capable of defining a factor.

Further Important Points about Factor Analyses

In test construction an item should load only 1 factor   Thus item 5 is problematic since it loads the extraversion factor as well as the neuroticism factor. However, this may be inevitable since neuroticism is associated with introversion (Eysenck, 1967a). Item 3 is problematic for inclusion in the final test because it loads its extraversion factor and factor 4. From the 10 items in Table 4.1 factor 4 cannot be interpreted since it has no items with high loadings on it. It is possible that from the whole pool the items loading on it had something in common, for example that they were all concerned with going to pubs. It would, therefore, be a very specific factor and of no interest to the test constructor other than as a warning that such items were not good for measuring personality.

Item 10 is a failure   This item fails to load any meaningful factor, and as has been said, it would have to be rejected.

Communality (h^2)   In our discussion of correlations in Chapter 3 it was pointed out that squaring them indicated how much common variance there was in the two variables. Thus the square of a factor loading shows how much variance the factor accounts for in an item. For example, factor 2 accounts for 56.25% of the variance in item 5. Given the unreliability of items, as discussed in Chapter 3, it suggests item 5 is a good item. If we square and add all the factor loadings for each item this gives us the communality which is, clearly, the total variance of an item which the factors explain. The four factors in Table 4.1 explain little of the variance in item 10 – hardly more than 10%.

Sums of squares, eigen values and percentage variance accounted for   Factors are described in terms of size, large and small. The size of a factor can be computed by squaring and adding its factor loadings (the sum of squares) and taking the average. Factor 1, for example, would entail the addition of .42, .65, .48 and the seven other loadings of factor 1 and dividing them by 10 (the number of variables). This computation yields the percentage of variance accounted for by the factor. In a good test the first factor should account for at least 60% of the variance among the items. Notice this still leaves considerable error. The raw sum of squares is referred to as the eigen value or the characteristic root.

More about eigen values   In the mathematics of factor analysis it is assumed that each variable (item in our example) has an eigen value of 1. Thus to be of any importance a factor must have an eigen value greater than 1. If it did not the factor would account for less variance than an item and would certainly be of no psychological or statistical importance. This must be so, given that a factor is a construct to simplify and account for the variance in correlation matrices. Indeed a factor can be seen as a sum of variables and thus its eigen value must be greater than 1, if it is not trivial. The percentage variance accounted (described above) is instantly recognisable as a measure of the importance of a factor but this index is correlated +1 with the eigen value, which itself indicates the importance of a variable. More will be said about eigen values later in this section.

The size of factors in factor analysis   In factor analysis, the aim is to simplify correlation matrices by working with a few factors which will explain much of the variance in the matrix. Test construction is a special case where, if we are constructing one test only, we require only one factor. Thus we want ideally a few large factors which explain most of the variance. In factor analysis the algebraic procedures of the methods (there are several kinds of factor analysis which will be described below) produce factors in order of decreasing size. Our main concern will be with the first few large factors (which usually account for most of the variance).

Negative loadings   It will be noted in our example in Table 4.1 that there were negative loadings. Negative loadings are just as important as positive loadings as the following example illustrates. Suppose we are factoring anxiety items. The item 'I feel anxious most of the time' scored 'Yes' would be expected to correlate positively with the anxiety factor accounting for much of the variance in the items. However, the item 'I am never afraid of danger' scored 'Yes' would have a negative correlation. This would still be a good anxiety item but it would be scored 'No' for the actual test score. Indeed all the signs of the factor loading could be reversed if we reversed the scoring, scoring the test for fearlessness. Then the first item would have a negative loading and the latter would be positive. Thus the sign of a loading does not diminish its psychological significance although, of course, it is critical for interpretation, as our example shows.

More General Points about Factor Analysis

Now that the most important technical terms of factor analysis have been discussed and explained I need to say more about what is actually done in carrying out a factor analysis. This will enable the reader to understand . factor analyses, as they are reported in research, and be in a position to appraise their worth. Again I shall eschew mathematics, although obviously for a full understanding of factor analysis the algebra must be grasped. There are many good texts elucidating factor analysis: Cattell (1978) is excellent, written by one of the great psychometrists, as is Harman (1976), but these are not easy books. Kline (1994) has written one of the most simplified accounts of factor analysis and this could prove helpful.

As has been discussed, it is the correlations between variables which are submitted to factor analysis. This involves several separate processes which are discussed below.

Initial condensation   The first computation of factor analysis is known as condensation, because it reduces the complexity of the correlation matrix by condensing the variables into factors. Remember that a factor is a sum of variables. It is important to note that there are different methods of condensation and these will be briefly described.

Principal components analysis   Principal components analysis analyses all the variance in the matrix. This has two interesting consequences: first, it means that error variance in the items is incorporated into the factors; and secondly, because all the variance is explained, it is difficult, in principle, to generalise from the results to another sample. Strictly, principal components analysis should be distinguished from factor analysis because there are as many components as variables. However, many of the factors are extremely small (eigen values less than 1) and these can be ignored. As Harman (1976) has shown, in large matrices the differences between principal components analysis and principal factor analysis are negligible and this has always been my experience.

Principal factor analysis   This is the most usual method of initial condensation. Its computation is virtually identical to that of principal components except that rather than assuming that each variable correlates perfectly with itself (without error) some estimate of its error is made. This means that in principal factor analysis error variance is not compounded with the factors which are hypothetical, estimated from the actual variables, in contrast to principal components. As discussed above, in practice there are few differences between factors and components.

Maximum likelihood analysis (MLA)   Maximum likelihood factor analysis is a relatively recent method for computing factors which produces estimates of the population factors from the sample correlation matrix. These maximum likelihood estimates can be tested for significance. This is the advantage of this method – that there is a statistical test for the number of factors, a problem with the other methods, as will be seen. In practice, however, with robust factors, maximum likelihood factor analysis gives results essentially identical to those of principal factors and components analysis.

Conclusions concerning initial methods of condensation   All methods in most circumstances give highly similar results. Because it has a statistical test for the number of factors, maximum likelihood analysis is in principle the best choice. However, for statistical reasons large samples are required for this procedure (>1000) and, as will be seen, there are problems with the statistical methods for selecting factors. Principal factors is often a convenient and easily comprehensible method.

Selecting the right number of factors   In our discussion of eigen values it was pointed out that factors are of unequal size. The smallest are trivial both psychologically and statistically. Thus it is necessary to decide how many factors are worthy of examination. Cattell (1978) has stressed the importance of selecting the correct number and various methods have been proposed. It is now generally agreed that if MLA has been used their statistical test should be followed, although with large samples it may be insensitive. With other methods of condensation the Scree test is a reliable method and many statistical computer packages have a program to this end.

The use of eigen values in selecting factors   Many computer packages have a default setting such that after the initial condensation, factors with eigen values greater than 1 are selected. The rationale for this has been explained: if the eigen value is greater than 1, the factor explains more variance than a variable. However, Cattell (1978) has shown that this often results in too many factors being selected and this is particularly so when factor analysis is used in test construction when there are usually many small factors.

Factor rotation: rotating the selected factors   In factor analysis, after the initial condensation and selection of factors and before any interpretation can be made, factors have to be rotated. Figure 4.1 illustrates a factor rotation.

Why factors have to be rotated: simple structure   Factors can be graphically represented as in Figure 4.1. As this figure makes clear the rotation of factors changes their loadings and each rotation or solution is mathematically equivalent. Thus in Figure 4.1 the stars represent the variables (items) in factor space. Variable *A* loads .3 on factor 1 and .35 on factor 2 (as a perpendicular line from the variable to each factor shows). However, by rotating factor 1 and factor 2 as in Figure 4.1 we have changed the loadings such that variable *A* now loads zero on factor 2 and .50 on factor 1. Of course these two factors could be rotated to any position and these are only two factors. The whole set of factors can be rotated to any position! Indeed there is an infinity of mathematically equivalent solutions to a factor analysis. Thurstone (1947) solved the problem of how to choose by arguing that the simplest solution was the best, what he called rotating to simple structure, which is obtained when each factor has a few high loadings with the majority being zero. Cattell (1978) has shown that simple structure yields replicable and meaningful factors and that this is the critical objective of good factor analysis. Actually it can be argued that that is an example

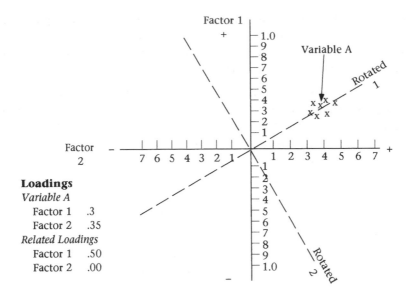

Figure 4.1   A rotated factor analysis

of Occam's razor, a principle in the natural sciences which claims that the simplest hypothesis is the best.

Obtaining simple structure   How simple structure may be obtained has been a matter of considerable debate. There are various different methods of rotation but one method has been shown to most reliably reach simple structure and that is the rotation known as Direct Oblimin (see Kline, 1994, 1999 for a full discussion of this point).

Oblique factors   Direct Oblimin produces oblique factors. These are correlated and the cosine of the angle between them indicates this correlation. Cattell (1978) has long argued that in the real world factors may well be correlated. However, it can be argued that correlated factors are not as simple as they might be.

Orthogonal Factors   These factors are uncorrelated and thus, possibly, more simple than any oblique set. If orthogonal simple structure is preferred the best rotation is Varimax. This and Direct Oblimin are available on most computer packages.

Interpreting the factors   It is the rotated factor analysis which must be interpreted.

Factor pattern and factor structure   In previous sections I defined factor loadings as correlations – the correlations of variables with the factors. This is true of unrotated factors which are orthogonal and orthogonal rotations. In oblique rotations there are two sets of factor loadings. The factor structure loadings are these correlations. The factor pattern loadings are beta weights. These weights are the weights that would be used in predicting each variable from the factors. When factors are uncorrelated the beta weights are the same as the correlations. When, in the oblique rotation, the factors are correlated, these beta weights take this correlation into account. It is easier to understand factors from their correlations, as was suggested. However, if the factors are highly correlated, the weights can be informative but such interpretation requires considerable experience of factor analysis.

A Summary of Factor Analysis

Subject the correlation matrix to initial condensation; select the salient factors; rotate factors; interpret the factor structure (or pattern if necessary).

Guidelines for Producing Good Factor Analyses

Cattell (1978) argued that many published factor analyses were misleading because they suffered from technical deficiencies, resulting in failure to reach simple structure. Even today, many factor analyses are technically deficient and to conclude this discussion of factor analysis some important points will be listed.

- Sample size. A minimum of 100 subjects is required. With smaller samples there is too much error in the correlation matrix.
- Subject to variable ratio. If there are more variables than subjects the factor analysis will be meaningless. Some authors have argued that a minimum ratio is 10:1 of subjects to variables. However, Barrett and Kline (1981b) showed that with clear factors a ratio of 2:1 yielded replicable results.
- Principal factors or MLA (if a large sample can be obtained) is best for the initial condensation.
- Factors should be selected by the Scree test or by statistical test if MLA has been used.
- Rotation to simple structure should be carried out by Varimax or Direct Oblimin, as best fits the data.
- All results should be replicated on new samples.

Use of Factor Analysis in Test Construction

This can be briefly set out in the context of our discussion of factor analysis.

- Administer the item pool to subjects, ensuring that the subject to variable ratio is satisfactory.
- Subject the item correlations to rotated simple structure factor analysis. Technically it is easier to construct several scales at once, using factor analysis. This is because rotation to simple structure minimises the general factor which is what is sought when only one scale is being constructed. With more than one scale this is a necessity, as has been discussed.
- Select items which load >.3 on one factor only. This eliminates the problem with item analysis that items loading correlated factors will correlate with the total score.
- Check that the successful items cover the gamut of the scale and write new items if required.
- Replicate the factor analysis on a new sample. Select the items which reach the criterion loading.
- Validate the scale and compute the reliability.

Conclusions

Tests constructed by technically adequate factor analyses, as described above, are bound to be univariate and reliable, although it is still necessary to validate the test, that is show what the factor is on which the items load. The majority of the best psychometric tests have been thus constructed.

Exploratory and Confirmatory Factor Analyses

I interrupted the description and discussion of factor analytic test construction with a lengthy diversion on factor analysis. As was then indicated this was done not only because factor analysis is complex and requires explication but also because factor analysis is used in psychometrics for far more than test construction. It is the statistical basis of many of the substantive discoveries of psychometrics in the field of ability and personality, which will be discussed in Chapters 5, 6 and 7.

So far in this discussion I have dealt with exploratory factor analysis where the aim of the analysis is to discover the main factors in the particular domain of investigation. For example, we could study the determinants of educational success by including measures of educational success together with tests of ability, assessments of school, teachers and home background. A factor analysis would efficiently reveal what variables were related to school success – all those loading the same factor as school success.

The vast majority of published factor analyses until the last few years were exploratory analyses. However, in recent years, thanks to the development of powerful computing packages, especially LISREL (Joreskog and Sorbom, 1984), confirmatory factor analyses are entering the field.

The mathematics of confirmatory analysis are formidable, although Kline (1994) has attempted a simple exposition, and readers are referred to that text. Loehlin (1987) has a brilliant account which is also accessible. Here, however, I shall set out the objectives of confirmatory factor analysis and discuss some of the problems which mean that results have to be treated with considerable caution.

Confirmatory Factor Analysis

In confirmatory factor analysis we hypothesise what the factor loadings ought to be, based upon previous work or psychological theory. The confirmatory factor analysis produces a factor analysis which fits these hypothesised loadings as closely as the actual data allow. If the fit is significant the hypothesis is confirmed. If no fit can be obtained, it is rejected. For example, we could hypothesise that a set of items measured three different personality traits and set their loadings accordingly. The confirmatory analysis could allow us to reject or accept the hypothesis.

All this sounds excellent and much more like the scientific method (to which hypothesis testing is central) than exploratory analyses in which researchers put in as many variables as possible and see what happens. However, as Loehlin (1987) has argued, there is a variety of problems which are usually ignored by enthusiasts for the method but which, as with exploratory analysis, can lead to delusion. These are set out below.

Setting out the target matrix   The set of hypothesised factor loadings is called the target matrix. If this were to be specified too precisely – each loading down to three decimal places, for example – it would be difficult to fit. For this reason it is common to specify a few loadings as high and the rest zero. This is a target which is not difficult to hit. Thus there are problems in specifying the target matrix.

Sample sizes   Confirmatory factor analysis uses maximum likelihood estimates for which large samples are required, as has been discussed. Many published studies are defective in this respect.

Indices of fit   Confirmatory factor analysis computes factor loadings to fit as closely as the data allow to the target matrix. To see whether they fit, there is a variety of statistical tests – indices of fit. However, these are not always in agreement with each other so that there is a problem concerning the fit of confirmatory factor analysis.

Sensitivity to sample size of indices of fit   There is a further problem with some of these indices. If the sample size is small, the indices tend to accept the hypothesised loading, even though visual inspection may suggest considerable discrepancies. When the sample size is large, as it ought to be, given the second point above, the indices tend to reject hypotheses, provided, on inspection, the fit appears to be good.

Meaning of fit   Even if all these difficulties are ignored there is the question of the meaning of the fact that the target matrix has been confirmed. That a hypothesis has been confirmed does not mean that there are not many other hypotheses which could have been confirmed. Thus confirmatory analysis is only one line of support for a hypothesis.

Conclusions   For all these reasons confirmatory analysis has to be used with great care. If we can specify a hypothesis, perhaps on theoretical grounds, and it is confirmed, this is useful supporting evidence but it must be remembered that hypotheses can never be proved by positive evidence. Logically they may only be refuted.

Constructing Tests using Item Characteristic Curves

This a method of test construction which I shall only discuss briefly since there are few psychological tests constructed from these curves, which are more fitted to the development of tests of knowledge. However, the advocates of this approach to test construction (for example, Embretson, 1996) have claimed that it is so superior to the conventional methods which have been described above that it should displace them. In fact this is certainly an exaggeration, for reasons which will be discussed below after the method has been described.

What is an Item Characteristic Curve?

An item characteristic curve indicates the probability of individuals at different levels of the variable being tested (the latent trait) passing the item. A typical item characteristic curve is set out in Figure 4.2.

The Latent Trait

The latent trait, which is highly similar to a factor, is notional and its meaning has to be inferred from the nature of the items, as is the case with a factor.

The Shape of the Curve

These item characteristic curves tend to the shape of the curve in Figure 4.2. This is a cumulative normal distribution, which is an assumption of item characteristic curve theory, to be discussed later in this section. Actually for ease of computation, it is assumed that these are logistic curves.

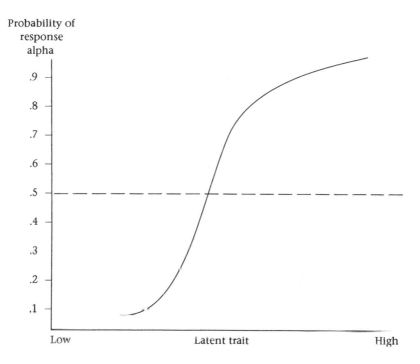

Figure 4.2   An item characteristic curve

Difficulty Level

This is defined as the point on the latent trait where the curve crosses the .5 probability. Clearly the further to the right this is on the graph, the more difficult the item.

Discriminating Power

The steeper the slope the more discriminating the item. This discrimination will be maximal among those individuals at the point on the latent trait where the item curve crosses the .5 level of probability.

Item Characteristic Curve Theory

Test construction using these item characteristic curves depends on item characteristic curve theory, which essentially consists of a number of models purporting to account for these item response curves which, of course, reflect how subjects respond to items. These models are highly similar to each other as Nunnally and Bernstein (1994) point out, and for this reason I shall briefly discuss one model which is not only one of the most simple but has other important characteristics. This is the Rasch model (Rasch, 1960).

The Rasch Model

The probability of a subject responding correctly to an item is a function of two variables: the facility of the item for eliciting the trait among subjects and the status of the subject on the latent trait. The facility of an item for eliciting the trait is equivalent to p, the difficulty level.

Comments on the Rasch Model

- Rasch scaled items are sample-free. The Rasch equations are claimed to yield sample-free indices of item difficulty, the facility of the item to elicit the trait. This means that Rasch-scaled items can be given to any subjects, regardless of their ability, and accurate scores will be obtained. This is quite different from classical test construction, where scores are distorted if the items are too hard or too easy.
- Subjects' scores are item-free. It follows from the above that the scores a subject obtains are not dependent on the particular set of items in the Rasch scale. Subsets of Rasch-scaled items will yield the same score for each subject.
- These are such powerful advantages of Rasch scaling, that any set of Rasch-scaled items will provide an accurate score for any subject, that it is pertinent to ask why there are so few Rasch scales.

Problems with Rasch Scales

I have discussed elsewhere (Kline, 1998, 1999) many of the difficulties with these scales and these are more technical than is fitting for this Primer. Here I shall summarise the most severe of these problems.

- To obtain sample-free scaling enormous samples have to be used (10 000 according to Lord, 1974).
- Chopin (1976) showed that it is difficult to obtain items which fitted the model, that is, would yield scales correctly measuring subjects at all levels of the trait.
- Wood (1978) fitted random data to the model.
- Barrett and Kline (1981a) Rasch scaled into one scale items from four scales, thus showing that fitting the Rasch model does not imply uni-dimensionality.
- The Rasch model does not fit the real world. This model implies a dimensionality such that high scorers score correctly all the items which lower scorers get correct. This may make sense for attainments but it does not do so for many psychological characteristics. In addition the model excludes guessing as a variable accounting for item response, although this can be incorporated.

- The model assumes that each item is perfectly correlated with the latent traits. In practice, given the notion of error and the imperfection of items, which factoring shows, this is simply not true.
- High correlation between Rasch scales and scales conventionally constructed. Nunnally (1978) showed that there was a high correlation between the two types of scale. This is hardly surprising because a conventional test can be Rasch scaled and many items will be retained.

Conclusions Concerning Rasch Scaling

Rasch scaling as method of test construction does not appear to have the outstanding advantages which have been claimed for it. For attainment tests where the knowledge has a clear structure so that more difficult items require that easier items are known, the Rasch model is at its most appropriate. If sufficient items can be written to fit the model then the pool of Rasch-scale items is valuable where retesting is necessary since subsets of items can be regarded as equivalent. However, for psychological variables, such as those of personality tests, where it is unreasonable to expect personality items to be ordered as demanded by the Rasch model, and where it is clear that the latent variable does not take up all the variance in the items, Rasch scaling would not appear to be, *a priori*, a useful method of test construction. Barrett (1998) contains an excellent critique of the Rasch model.

The Rasch Model as an Example of Conjoint Measurement

In Chapter 2, I discussed the differences between psychometric and scientific measurement. It was noted that scientific measures were ratio scales with clear units of measurement and true zeros, characteristics which conventional psychometric tests did not possess. However Wright (1985) has argued that Rasch scales are, in fact, examples of simultaneous conjoint measurement, a point emphasised by Michell (1990, 1997). As Luce and Tukey (1964) demonstrated, quantitative structure exists in such conjoint measures. Thus, Rasch scales are examples of genuine scientific measurement and for this reason they should be the preferred method of test construction. Their advantages as conjoint measures ought to outweigh the problems with scaling which were raised above.

Simultaneous Conjoint Measurement

As was discussed in Chapter 2 conjoint measurement requires that a score on a variable is a function of two other independent variables. Of course, this is indeed the case with Rasch scales, although only in the simple model without a guessing parameter, since response to an item is a function of the position of a subject on the latent trait, and the facility of the item in eliciting the trait. However, as I have fully discussed in Kline (1998) I believe these arguments in favour of Rasch scales are mistaken. I shall exemplify the points by referring to tests of extraversion.

The Latent Trait   The variance in the items must be accounted for by subjects' position on the latent trait (plus the facility level of the item). However, we do not know what this latent trait is. We do know from factoring items that items do not just load their factor, thus this latent trait could not be a pure measure of extraversion and, as has been discussed, fitting the Rasch model does not guarantee unidimensionality. Thus the latent trait in Rasch scaling is not a pure measure.

Units of measurement   Rasch scaling is said to provide units of measurement and thus equal intervals. It does so by scaling the difficulty level of the items independently of the sample taking the test. However, this means that there are equal intervals among the items forming the scale but this does not mean that the items are forming equal intervals of extraversion. It would be incredible to believe that a set of Rasch-scaled personality test items formed units of measurement. What are these units? The same is true for intelligence tests.

Final Conclusions Concerning Rasch Scaling and Other Methods of Test Construction

These arguments seem to me to demonstrate that Rasch scaling is not the answer to the demands for ratio scales with units of measurement. Their units crucially are different from those of the measures in the natural sciences and the latent traits are unknown and not unitary. Rasch scales can provide, especially for attainment tests, accurate scaling of items such that subsets of items can be used for testing, which has definite advantages in the applied field. Indeed, if the items are presented on a computer, the Rasch indices can be used to tailor a set of items precisely to the abilities of an individual, a procedure known as adaptive or tailored testing, although, strictly, with Rasch indices such item selection is unnecessary. However, for most psychological tests, this method of test construction offers little advantage over conventional methods. Of these, factor analysis, provided that it is technically sound, is likely to yield the best tests in terms of reliable, univariate measures, although in many cases item analysis is effective. However, with computing resources so easily available, item analysis has no advantages over factor analysis, as was once the case. Criterion keying is not a method to be used unless a quick screening is the sole aim of the test.

5
Intelligence and Ability Tests

Introduction

In our discussion of factor analysis in Chapter 4 it was pointed out that factor analysis was used in psychometrics far more than test construction. Indeed it is the statistical technique with which psychometrics has made its substantive discoveries and this is particularly the case in the field of abilities and intelligence.

Definition of Abilities

Abilities I define here as the cognitive traits implicated in solving problems. The term cognitive refers to information processing. Traits which involve information processing are described as cognitive. This is important since the solution of problems, particularly difficult and complex problems, involves other traits such as persistence, for example, which are attributes of personality, as will be discussed in Chapter 6. Intelligence is defined, essentially as did Spearman (1904), as a general reasoning ability, general because it is applicable to problems in many different fields. This, it should be made clear, is not simply my idiosyncratic definition but is the one adopted by most of the leading psychometrists, for example Cattell (1971), Jensen (1980), Carroll (1993) and Mackintosh (1998).

Ever since Spearman (1904) demonstrated that a general factor (g) could account for performance in a wide variety of tasks together with factors specific to each task, psychometrists have used factor analysis to tease out the nature of human abilities. The general approach which has been used is to administer a battery of tests covering the spectrum of abilities and to submit the correlations to factor analysis. Over the years there have been many different factorial accounts of human abilities, two of the most famous and distinctive being the single general factor, plus specifics, of Spearman, and Thurstone's (1947) nine-factor solution, from which the general factor appeared to be missing. These two disparate accounts were reconciled by Vernon (1961) who proposed a hierarchical solution in which general ability was at the top accounting for a number of group factors, for example verbal ability and spatial ability which in turn accounted for some smaller, more specific factors, for example grammatical reasoning and vocabulary, in the case of verbal ability. The distinguished psychometrist Guilford (1967), on the other hand, proposed a far more complex account of the factor analysis of abilities embracing no fewer than 120 factors.

As was discussed in Chapter 4, Cattell (1978) had argued that many of the disagreements of factor analysis were due to technical deficiencies which had prevented the authors from obtaining simple structure. In a previous study of human abilities Cattell (1971) postulated on the basis of a full sampling of human abilities and technically correct simple structure factor analyses that there were 21 clear primary ability factors at the first order and that when the correlation between these were subjected to factor analysis – second-order factor analysis – 5 clear factors accounted for the variance in human abilities of which the two largest were crystallised and fluid ability. These two factors which are correlated are equivalent to the old Spearman's g.

My own research into the factorial structure of human abilities has always found support for this Cattellian position (for example Kline and Cooper, 1984a) and it was confirmed, almost beyond question (although science is always ready for disconfirmation, unlike the dogmas of religion and the social sciences), by the work of Carroll (1993). He factored the original data of the vast majority of published studies of human abilities using the best factor analytic procedures (see Chapter 4) and his list of factors may be regarded as definitive. However, it is essentially identical to that of Cattell (1971). These factors will form the basis of the discussion in this chapter. However, despite this impressive agreement concerning the factor analysis of human abilities there are still a few writers, for example Gardner (1983), who attempt to argue for what they refer to as multiple intelligences.

In this chapter, therefore, I shall set out the main ability factors, including intelligence, and explicate their psychological meaning. In the light of this discussion other accounts of intelligence and ability will be evaluated. The tests from which these factors are derived will be described, and finally I shall summarise some of the main findings concerning the development and inheritance of intelligence and ability.

The Primary Ability Factors

The factors set out in Table 5.1 are those on which there is a general agreement in the most comprehensive and careful studies, including those of Cattell (1971), Carroll (1993) and Ekstrom, et al. (1976).

Table 5.1   The main primary ability factors

V	verbal ability: understanding words and ideas.
N	numerical factor: facility in the manipulation of numbers (not arithmetic reasoning).
S	spatial ability: ability to recognise figures in different orientations.
P	perceptual speed and accuracy: rapidly assessing differences between stimuli.
Cs	speed of closure: ability to complete a pattern with a part missing.
I	inductive reasoning.
Ma	rote memory: memorising unlinked stimuli.
Mk	mechanical ability.
Cf	flexibility of closure: ability to find stimuli among distractors.
Ms	memory span: ability to recall immediately lists of letters or digits.
Sp	spelling.
E	aesthetic judgement: ability to detect the basic principles of good art.
Mm	meaningful memory: ability to learn links between linked stimuli.
O1	originality of ideational flexibility: ability to generate many different and original ideas.
Fl	ideational fluency: ability rapidly to develop many ideas on a topic.
W	word fluency: rapid production of words according to letter requirements.
O2	originality: this is derived from the task of combining two objects into one functional object.
A	aiming: hand–eye co-ordination.
Rd	representational drawing ability.
Au	auditory ability: ability to differentiate between and remember a sequence of tones.

There are some important points which must be noted about this table.

- This is not the definitive list of factors. As Cattell (1971) stressed, the production of a definitive list of factors is virtually impossible. These primary factors in Table 5.1 account for most of the variance in the main tests of ability. However, many variables have never been tested – especially those not included in current school curricula – the ability to understand animals, to detect hidden sources of food, to track in the jungle, for example. Furthermore it is possible to break down abilities into smaller and smaller subsections and, with enough items for each, a factor could be produced. A good example of this can be found in musical ability and tests have been constructed which measure tone discrimination, rhythm perception, chordal perception and so on (for example, Seashore, 1919). However, as Carroll (1993) demonstrated, these are the factors which reliably appear, when all studies are subjected to technically correct factor analysis.
- Factor analysis was developed to simplify the field when very large numbers of variables are involved. However, the 20 factors of Table 5.1 are still too many to take in and hold easily in one's mind.

Nevertheless the comments below on some of these factors will be useful for our later discussion of intelligence and ability.

- Verbal ability. It should come as no surprise that this is an important ability factor. It clearly varies enormously, from poets and writers to the virtually tongue-tied. Furthermore it is difficult to see how complex ideas can be understood unless verbal ability is highly developed (with the possible exception of mathematical ideas). Indeed, Robinson (1999) has suggested that verbal ability is at the heart of intelligence, a viewpoint which will be examined later in this chapter.

- N, the numerical factor. This is highly interesting, because this ability to manipulate numbers, which is so marked in some individuals but weak in so many, hence the need for calculators, is independent of mathematical ability which is far more a matter of mathematical reasoning. This is much more associated with I, inductive reasoning.

- Perceptual speed and accuracy. This is another interesting factor, which raises, as does factor N above, the question of speed and intelligence. Carroll (1993) has claimed, for example, that many intelligence tests are confounded by this variable of speed which should be separated out. However, a recent study by Draycott and Kline (1996) showed clearly that this mental or cognitive speed factor was separate from measures of intelligence.

- Speed and power tests. This brief mention of speed is a convenient point to bring up the distinction between speed and power tests. A power test is given untimed, whereas, as the name suggests, there is time limit for speeded tests. Most intelligence tests and ability tests are thus speed tests. However, there is a high correlation between the same test, timed and untimed (Vernon, 1961).

- I, inductive reasoning. As was discussed at the beginning of this chapter, intelligence is defined as a general reasoning ability. Thus of all these primary factors, this factor of inductive reasoning is most close to intelligence defined in this way.

- Memory factors. It is to be noted that there are three memory factors. This supports the detailed experimental study of memory by cognitive psychologists (for example, Baddeley, 1990) who regard memory as a complex cognitive process, utilising various buffers, stores and labels. It is clear that it is convenient to think of short-term memory, as when we memorise a telephone number when dialling the number and long-term memory into which that number will not go unless it is regularly used. This is mentioned here because short-term memory or working memory is essential for problem solving and one researcher has attempted to identify it with intelligence (Kyllonen and Christal, 1990), although this would appear to be going beyond the evidence.

- These factors are virtually identical to those extracted by Cattell (1971) and with the exception of O1, they can be tested by the Comprehensive Ability Battery (CAB) (Hakstian and Cattell, 1976).
- These primary ability factors are correlated. It is important to note that these factors are not independent. There are positive correlations between them.
- Conclusions concerning these primary factors. These factors support common-sense notions of human ability that individuals vary on verbal and reasoning ability and that some people are quick in thinking and others slow. However, there are still too many to be able to make a coherent picture of human ability from them. Fortunately, as mentioned above, these are correlated. Hence Table 5.1 can be further simplified by factor analysis of the correlations between the factors (second-order factors) and by yet further factor analysis of the correlations between the second orders (third-order analysis). Such analyses ought to simplify the field yet further and the results of these are set out in Table 5.2.

Table 5.2   The main higher-order ability factors

---

1   g (third order). This was extracted from around 150 of the data sets by Carroll (1993).
2   Fluid intelligence. This is a second-order factor which emerged from most of the data sets in the study by Carroll, as did all the factors in Table 5.2.
3   Crystallised intelligence.
4   Visual perception.
5   Auditory perception.
6   Cognitive speed.
7   Retrieval ability.
8   Memory ability.

Discussion of Table 5.2

To account for the differences in human ability with seven factors (the third-order factor g summarises the seven, as will be seen) is clearly a real simplification. I shall now describe these factors and make other relevant comments in the light of the evidence about them. It must be remembered that factors are identified from their loadings and that second-order factors have their loadings on the primaries described in Table 5.1. The third-order factor loads, of course, the second orders.

A General Comment Concerning Table 5.2

Five of these second-order factors are identical to those of Cattell (1971): fluid and crystallised ability, cognitive speed, the retrieval factor and visualisation. Furthermore it must be pointed out that Cattell was responsible for the discovery and investigation of fluid and crystallised ability which he developed into his investment theory of intelligence. Thus these second-order factors which Carroll demonstrated were to be found in the majority of factor analytic studies of intelligence, a striking testament to Cattell's (1971) work on human abilities.

Fluid Intelligence

As Cattell (1971) demonstrated, the original g factor of Spearman on proper rotation broke down into two correlated factors – fluid and crystallised intelligence. Fluid intelligence is the basic reasoning ability of the brain, largely genetically determined, according to Cattell, representing the neural efficiency of the brain.

Crystallised Intelligence

This is the ability in the set of skills most valued in a culture. At the turn of the century in the West this was Classics and Mathematics and these subjects loaded highly on intelligence tests. Today technological subjects, computing and physics, have to some extent taken their place.

Relation of Fluid and Crystallised Intelligence

According to Cattell, fluid intelligence is invested in these skills. Thus in adult life there is a positive moderate correlation between fluid and crystallised intelligence. This correlation is, for obvious reasons, at its highest in infancy and early childhood and it then decreases, depending on the cultural stimulation available to the child and to some extent in personality factors. Thus compliant children, who accept the mores of a middle-class home and school, are likely to invest much of their fluid intelligence in culturally approved ways. Thus their crystallised intelligence will reflect accurately their fluid ability. This may account for the recent findings that girls are out-performing boys in academic subjects. Warburton (1965) showed, for example, that in a group of psychopathic criminals fluid ability was far higher than crystallised ability, a finding which is mirrored in studies of disadvantaged children. Indeed, as Cattell and Johnson (1986) argue, it is valuable in working with children with educational problems to be able to measure fluid and crystallised intelligence separately.

Conclusions Concerning the Intelligence Factors

In the light of this factor analytic research it is strictly incorrect to talk of intelligence. Intelligence is comprised of two factors: fluid intelligence, the basic capacity of the brain to reason, and crystallised intelligence, that capacity as it is evinced in solving problems in fields thought valuable in a culture. Intelligence, as measured by many intelligence tests, is a mixture of these two factors, although these may be, and ought to be, separately measured. Of course any real life problem solving reflects a subject's status on both these factors, which is why it is convenient still to use the term intelligence. Finally it must be pointed out that in any battery of cognitive tests these two factors account for much of the variance. For the prediction of problem-solving ability these two factors are the most useful.

Other Second-Order Factors

These can be dealt with far more briefly, because although they account for some variance in human abilities, they are less significant than the two intelligence factors, being narrower and more specialised.

- Visual perception, or visualisation, as it was named by Cattell (1971), refers to ability to visualise which is important in the solution of some kinds of problem. For example, many statisticians, expert in multivariate analysis and factor analysis, seem to have little problem in visualising N dimensional space and this same ability is obviously valuable for architects and engineers. The first-order spatial ability factor loads this visual factor.
- Cognitive speed. This factor can be seen in such activities as writing and mental arithmetic. Some individuals are rapid at everything they do and this reflects their status on this factor.
- Retrieval capacity. This is a fluency factor, reflecting the ability to retrieve material quickly from memory. When found in subjects of mediocre intelligence it can lead to the boring, mindless verbosity which characterises chat-show chair people.
- The memory factor. According to Carroll (1993) this is involved in any task in which memorising plays a part. Similarly the auditory perception factor is involved in all tasks requiring auditory discrimination, in ordinary life, mainly tasks in learning and performing music.

Conclusions Concerning the Second-Order Factors

Second-order factor analysis has neatly summarised the nature of human ability. Two large factors, fluid and crystallised intelligence, pervade the performance of most tasks. Retrieval capacity is important as regards fluency, which may be useful in creative performance (Guilford, 1967). Cognitive speed and visualisation are also important in certain problems as are auditory perception and various kinds of memory factors. There can be no doubt from these analyses that the first two factors, the split of the old g factor, are essential in problem solving.

The Third-Order g Factor

Although third-order factors are, in principle, derived from the correlations between second-order factors it is possible and usually more informative to compute the loadings of primary factors on the third orders. The third order g factor, in the work of Carroll (1993), when submitted to this form of analysis, has highly informative loadings, the main ones being induction, visualisation, quantitative reasoning and verbal ability. This factor, therefore, is truly general and loads all those variables which we would regard as typical of intelligence. For this reason it has been identified as a general reasoning factor, as postulated by Spearman (1904), by Undheim (1981) and Undheim and Gustafsson (1987). This broad general factor accounts for a considerable proportion of the variance in human abilities, more at the lower levels than at the higher (Deary et al., 1996). However, it is so broad that for many measurement purposes it makes more sense to measure the primary or secondary factors which it embraces. Nevertheless the existence of this factor is further support for the notion of a general reasoning ability, as are the correlated factors of fluid and crystallised intelligence.

Brief Comments on some other Accounts of Human Abilities

As was discussed in Chapter 4, rotation to simple structure was shown by Cattell (1978) to lead to meaningful and replicable factors. Hence it was no surprise that the enormous survey of Carroll (1993) confirmed his factor analysis of human abilities. Nevertheless there are still some authors who attempt to put a different case and whose work is still cited. Two such analyses I shall discuss briefly below.

The Work of Guilford

Guilford (1967) and Guilford and Hoepfner (1971) made extensive factor analytic studies of human abilities which resulted in the Structure of Intellect Model which included 120 ability factors. This model was notable for a number of reasons, particularly because it denied the claim that human abilities are all positively correlated (Guilford, 1964), because its factors were orthogonal, on the ground that orthogonal factors were more simple, *per se*, than oblique sets, and because it laid emphasis on the distinction between convergent thinking (as measured by intelligence tests) and divergent thinking which Guilford argued was more useful for creative problem solving. The importance of this model in understanding human abilities is that the notion of a general ability is abandoned. Abstract thinking ability is just one of many factors.

There have been many objections to this model, such as that its provenance is quite arbitrary, being rooted neither in factor analytic results nor in theoretical cognitive psychology, as Eysenck (1967b) and Cattell (1971) have argued. However, I shall not detail these arguments because there is a more fundamental and empirical objection to this work. I suggested above that this model was not based on factor analytic results. This is correct in that Guilford and his colleagues did not carry out extensive exploratory analyses and discover 120 factors which they were forced to introduce into their model. On the contrary, the model was developed and factor analyses were computed to fit the model. In Chapter 4 we discussed confirmatory analysis as a method of supporting factor analytic hypotheses. Guilford used Procrustes analyses to fit target matrices which essentially stretch or compress the variance (hence the name) to fit the targets. In this way Guilford was able to support 98 of these factors and there was every hope with the development of new tests that the remainder would be confirmed. However, unfortunately for the Structure of Intellect Model, Horn and Knapp (1973) showed that Procrustes rotations could not reject targets, regardless of the original matrices, and this finding destroys the empirical support for the Guilford model.

The Work of Gardner

Gardner (for example, 1983), who is not in the factor analytic tradition, has argued that the notion of g, as general intelligence, is incorrect but that there are many intelligences of which high reasoning ability is only one, musical and linguistic intelligences being others. This research was based upon the study of small numbers of gifted individuals and in such a sample the influence of general ability is bound to be less than within the normal range. For example, Beethoven was highly intelligent but few would argue that this was the major contributing ability to his genius. In fact, as the work of Cattell (1971) and Carroll (1993) shows there is no real contradiction between Gardner's findings and the factor analytic work. Of course these special factors are important in gifted individuals. However, ability factors are correlated and there are two factors of general intelligence (or one at the third order). What is incorrect about Gardner's claims is the inference that there is no important general factor or factors. This cannot be supported from his findings with specialised samples or from the 10 000 or so studies surveyed by Carroll (1973).

Conclusions Concerning the Structure of Human Abilities

The factor analytic findings are remarkably clear. Two general reasoning factors account for much of the variance in human ability: fluid and crystallised intelligence. There are other substantial factors including vis-ualisation, cognitive speed and retrieval capacity. Other primary factors of smaller variance can be isolated. The importance of the general factors does not deny the influence in some individuals of more specific abilities such as musical ability or high visualisation, as in chess players, for example. The single most important finding which is replicated again and again over almost 100 years and in 10 000 studies is the pervasive influence of general ability as evinced in fluid and crystallised intelligence.

Intelligence Testing and the Nature of Human Intelligence

Having described the findings from the factor analysis of human abilities, I shall now examine the nature of intelligence as it is revealed in the study of these factors. These discussions will not only cast light on the factor analytic picture of intelligence but in so doing will provide evidence for the validity of the psychometric test of intelligence on which they are based. These tests will then be briefly described.

Over the 95 years since factor analytic g was first described there has been a vast outpouring of research into the nature of the general factor, or factors. This work has been theoretical on the structure of abilities, which has been described, and practical where intelligence tests have been used in occu-pational, clinical and educational psychology. I intend to summarise briefly the psychological significance of all this work. This huge task has been made easier by some brilliant summaries and surveys of such research, especially Jensen (1998), Brody (1992), Saklofske and Zeidner (1995), Gottfredson (1997a) in a special issue of the journal *Intelligence* and Mackintosh (1998), although the arguments here are those of the present author. Kline (1998, 1999) has delineated some of these points in greater detail. Finally it should be noted that in the discussion I shall deal with fluid and crystallised intel-ligence together as if they were one factor, except where stated.

- Intelligence and academic success. As Gottfredson (1997a) points out it may be regarded as demonstrated that scores on intelligence tests correlate with academic performance at all ages. Caution has to be shown about the exact size of the correlation because correlations can be attenuated in studies of this sort by two factors: the unreliability of academic exams and the homogeneity of samples, especially with students in Higher Education. Despite this, impressive results have been obtained. In the work of Terman and Oden (1959) who studied children of high IQ, measured at five years of age, this score was a good predictor of future academic performance. Vernon (1960) demonstrated that the correlation between intelligence and performance at the primary school was around .6. It is a good predictor of secondary school academic attainment and performance at university because, as Jensen (1980) argues, intelligent children simply learn more quickly than less able children.

- Intelligence, academic success and a third variable. It has been argued by opponents of intelligence tests that the correlation discussed above is created by the effects of some third variable or variables which affects both academic attainment and intelligence – poor environment or lack of parental encouragement. This depends on the claim that intelligence is simply an attainment – learning to reason. This argument will not do. Vernon (1960) showed that practice in intelligence tests produced only small gains and these were quickly realised after a few hours. Furthermore such gains did not generalise to intelligence tests which were not practised. In addition this argument fails to account for the fact that there are differences in intelligence test scores among children reared in similar environments. Attainment, on the other hand, clearly does reflect practice as Ericsson (1988) has demonstrated and as every teacher and learner knows.

- Motivation as third variable. Some have argued that the correlation between intelligence and attainment reflects motivation to perform well. In the light of the psychometric evidence such claims are hopeless. First, Cattell (1957, 1971) showed that motivational and personality variables accounted for different aspects of the variance in academic success. Furthermore were this argument sound the correlation between each subject in the curriculum and intelligence would be the same. This, however, as Jensen (1980) has shown, is not the case. The more complex the subject, the higher the correlation with g (Gottfredson, 1997a). For example, mathematics and classics have high correlations with g, while sociology and the social sciences have far lower correlations.

- The common content of intelligence tests and academic attainment. It has been argued that the correlation between intelligence test scores and attainment reflects some common content between the two. Although, as shall be seen, such a claim is difficult to sustain in the light of the nature of intelligence tests it is refuted by the fact that the best predictor of ability at an entirely new subject is the intelligence test.

- Conclusions. This correlation between intelligence tests and academic attainment can be explained most parsimoniously by conceptualising intelligence as the ability to reason.

- Intelligence and occupational success. I shall deal only briefly with this topic since it will be an important aspect of Chapter 8. However, no lengthy treatment is required because there are clear and unequiv-ocal findings. Ghiselli (1966), in a survey of 10 000 studies, showed that the single best predictor for any job was the intelligence test and the average correlation was .3. These findings have been replicated by Gottfredson (1986, 1997b) and Furnham (1995). Again all this supports the notion that intelligence, as measured by intelligence tests, is general reasoning ability.

The Heritability of Intelligence Test Scores

The heritability of a trait refers to the extent to which it is genetically determined. Eye and hair colour are entirely thus determined as is gender, whereas some traits such as intelligence appear to be determined by both genetic and environmental factors. This is a contentious topic with strong political overtones and it is noteworthy that although in principle this is an empirical matter, in practice left-wing psychologists minimise the influence of genetic factors and vice versa. In this discussion I shall attempt to be entirely objective.

The findings concerning the heritability of intelligence have been obtained from the biometric analysis of intelligence test scores and although the mathematics of this are complex and beyond the scope of this Primer, the principles are clear and logical and these will be explicated. In addition I shall stress a few other essential points before discussing the results which are remarkably unequivocal.

- What is biometric analysis? This involves the study of the correlations, strictly variances and covariances (see Chapter 4 and Glossary), of a set of scores, any score, not just intelligence, of individuals of varying degrees of relatedness. An example will clarify the method. Monozygotic (MZ) twins are genetically identical, in contrast to dizygotic twins (DZ) who have, like ordinary siblings, half their genes in common. Thus with a genetically determined trait, there would be no differences between the members of each MZ pair. The more this intra-pair correlation departs from 1 the greater the environmental determination. Environmentally determined variance, it should be noted, can be itself broken down into two sources: common and unique variance. From this several simple inferences can be made. MZ twins should have a higher correlation for a heritable trait than DZ twins. The difference in correlation between MZ twins reared together and MZ twins reared apart must indicate the influence of the envir-onment. Obviously comparisons between pairs of different degrees of relatedness – siblings, cousins, half siblings, parent–child, adopted and biological parent–child, taking into account whether they were reared together or apart, are all of great interest. Biometric analysis has developed formal methods for such analyses (see Fulker, 1979 for a clear description).

- The meaning of heritability coefficients. The results of biometric analysis set out the proportion of variance determined by genetic factors and by environmental factors. For example, some studies show that 60% of the variance in intelligence test scores is determined by genetic factors. This refers to the variance in the population which was sampled in the particular research. In populations with only slight variance in the environment genetic determination is bound to be higher than in those with considerable environmental fluctuations. The environmental variance is split between common variance, that which applies to all members of a family and the unique variance which is different for each member of the family.
- The results of the biometric analysis of intelligence tests. Here I shall indicate the most psychologically meaningful results of this research. Good summaries can be found in Mackintosh (1998) and Plomin and Petrill (1997).
- Correlations betwee MZ twins reared apart and together and DZ twins under these conditions. Pedersen et al. (1992) studied all adult twins reared apart in Sweden. The correlations are set out in Table 5.3.

Table 5.3 Correlations of adult twins reared together and apart

MZ together .80	MZ apart .78
DZ together .32	DZ apart .22

- Comments on Table 5.3. There can be no doubt that the intelligence test scores in this study are highly heritable. If this were not so there would be no differences between the sets of twins.
- Heritability of intelligence increases with age. By adulthood the influence of the environment on intelligence test scores is low. In this Swedish study there was no correlation between environmental differences in the separated twins and differences within the pairs. This is supported by studies of adopted children where the correlation between the adopted child and adopted parent sinks to zero in adulthood.
- Brody and Crowley (1995) point out that a shared environment is not influential in the determination of intelligence. The shared environment refers to factors such as education and social class and this runs contrary to much sociological theorising. The important environmental

determinants appear to be the unique variance, the factors affecting specifically each child in the family.

- Gene loci in the inheritance of intelligence. With the rapid development of the study of the human genome, in principle at least, it should become possible to isolate the genes which actually produce differences in intelligence. A start has been made on this work. Skuder et al. (1995) found a gene associated with high IQ but in a recent paper Petrill et al. (1996) were unable to replicate this finding. However, these are early days in the search for genetic markers and there seems little doubt that the relevant genes will be found.

- Conclusions. These findings, which are typical of the biometric research and are not exceptional or unusual, demonstrate that intelligence test scores are highly heritable. There is no sensible way to account for the correlations between pairs of DZ and MZ twins and children with their adopted and biological parents. Of course, not all the variance is accounted for. What the environmental determinants are has yet to be determined empirically. They could be physiological factors, influencing the prenatal development of the child, a possibility since obvious psychological influences such as verbal stimulation and targeted educational programmes have disappointingly little effect (Jensen, 1998). A final possibility is that psychometric tests are somewhat errorful measures of intelligence, as is suggested by our earlier discussions on the nature of scientific measurement in Chapter 2. This is the area, along with the study of genetic markers for future research, on which future research must concentrate.

The Nature of Psychometric Intelligence

Intelligence as measured by intelligence tests has been clearly illuminated by the research which has been discussed in the previous sections. It is a factor which predicts academic performance and occupational success better than any other variable. In addition it is a highly heritable factor. All this fits well with the concept of intelligence as a general reasoning ability suitable for problem solving in almost any sphere.

Psychometric Tests of Intelligence

In this chapter our study of psychometric intelligence will be completed by an examination and scrutiny of intelligence tests. I shall not describe the items in any particular test because these must be kept confidential. Obviously tests would lose their validity if the items were known. This is not, as some have attempted to claim, an indictment of intelligence tests. The rationale of these tests is that the items sample the problem-solving ability of the subjects taking the test. If these have seen the items before, the basis of the test is removed.

It will become obvious, from the items used in tests, that these measure reasoning ability, as they were designed to do. However, it must be remembered that face validity (see Chapter 3) is not a good guide to true validity. However, since this has been demonstrated for intelligence tests it is reasonable to examine their items.

Group and Individual Tests of Intelligence

Intelligence tests fall into two groups, those designed to test subjects individually and those which can be used with groups of subjects. Individual tests are used in educational psychology where it is useful to observe how the child actually goes about solving the problems. However, they take about an hour to administer and require specialised training. Group tests need far less skill to administer and where large numbers of subjects need to be tested these are generally used.

Individual Tests

The two most well-known individual tests of intelligence are two of the oldest, although they have been extensively modified and developed over the years. These are regarded as benchmark measures of intelligence, although they were developed before the structure of abilities was defined. In fact they measure a mixture of crystallised and fluid intelligence. These are the tests devised by David Wechsler – the Wechsler scales for adults and children – and the Stanford–Binet test which was a development of the original work on intelligence by Binet and Simon (1905).

The Wechsler Scales (Wechsler, 1958)

The reference refers to the book on the appraisal of intelligence. The actual tests are updated regularly and the most recent editions are obtainable from the Psychological Corporation. Full details of the Wechsler scales can be found in Kline (1999). Different scales are available allowing the testing of children as young as three years of age and onwards to adulthood. I shall restrict my discussion to the adult scale (WAIS) which fully typifies the whole set.

In the WAIS there are ten scales divided into two groups, verbal and non-verbal.

Verbal scales

- Information. This tests general knowledge. The rationale is that intelligent individuals know more because they are quick learners (Jensen, 1980).
- Comprehension. This tests the ability to go to the heart of a problem by presenting subjects with questions requiring the explanation of the meanings of proverbs and the purposes of legislation, for example.
- Arithmetic. This tests simple arithmetic ability of the traditional kind.
- Similarities. This requires subjects to explain in what way two things are similar. The correct score is obtained by explicating the essence of the similarity rather than some superficial aspect. For example, the similarity between a sweetcorn and a yellow pepper would not be colour but the fact that they were both vegetables.
- Vocabulary. This is a standard vocabulary test. As Vernon (1960) showed it is the single best test of crystallised intelligence although at an early age vocabulary loads fluid intelligence.
- Digit span. In digit span subjects are required to read out a string of digits immediately after reading. In addition there is backward digit span where the digits have be read in reverse order.

Comments on the verbal tests of the WAIS   It is clear from our description of these tests that these are measures of crystallised intelligence, with the exception of digit span. This is supported by the many factor analyses of the WAIS of which that reported by Woliver and Saeks (1986) is particularly clear. That digit span should load fluid intelligence (even moderately) is interesting from the viewpoint of understanding this factor. As the cognitive studies of Baddeley (1990) indicate, an efficient and capacious working memory is essential for problem solving, and the memory factor is naturally the main factor on which digit span loads.

Performance Scales

- Digit symbol. In this test digits and symbols are shown together. With this chart before them subjects have to fill in the correct symbols for the digits, as quickly as possible for this is a speeded test.
- Picture completion. In this test pictures are shown to subjects who are required within 20 seconds to indicate what is missing.
- Block design. In this test subjects are given patterns which they have to make by putting blocks together.

- Picture arrangement. Here each item consists of a sequence of pictures which has to be arranged in an order which tells a story.
- Object assembly. This test is essentially a jigsaw in which the pieces have to be correctly assembled as quickly as possible.

Comments on the performance scales   Cattell (1971) claimed that the best tests of fluid ability were of two kinds: those that used items which were equally unfamiliar to all subjects and those with items that were completely part of everyone's culture. The performance scales fall into these groups and it is unlikely that the performance scales would be affected by social class and education to the same extent as the verbal scales. From the nature of these scales loadings on fluid ability and cognitive speed factors would be expected.

Comments on the WAIS Test as a Whole

This test is regarded as a benchmark measure of intelligence. New tests of intelligence are validated against its scores although it was constructed before the factor analysis of abilities was clearly elucidated. In fact, as the work of Woliver and Saeks (1986) shows, the verbal scales load crystallised intelligence and the performance scales fluid intelligence. As was mentioned above, perceptual and cognitive speed are also involved in some of the scales.

This analysis indicates why the WAIS is a good predictor of real-life intelligence because this latter is a mixture of the two intelligence factors, as is the test. In educational psychology it is instructive to note when there is considerable discrepancy between the performance and the verbal scales. Superiority in the latter may indicate a modest ability with an excellent educational background. The opposite case may show that a child is not making the most of her abilities.

Other Individual Tests of Intelligence

The Stanford–Binet test is similar to the Wechsler tests although it was designed primarily for children and there are usually insufficient items at the top end of the scale for bright adults. It differs from the Wechsler scales in that the items are arranged by level of difficulty rather than by item type and only one score, the IQ, is obtained. This is almost certainly crystallised intelligence since the vocabulary score on this test, the best measure of crystallised intelligence, correlated very highly with the total score on the test (Cattell and Johnson, 1986).

Finally mention should be made of the more modern British Ability Scale (BAS) first developed at Manchester by Elliot (1983). This has many scales designed to test individual abilities and was based on the work of Piaget and Guilford, although customer demand enables a traditional IQ to be scored.

Group Tests

There is a large number of group tests of intelligence. For a full list readers must be referred to Bartram et al. (1992). Here I shall briefly describe and discuss the most valid measures.

Raven's Matrices (Raven, 1965c)

These were developed by Raven in the late 1930s and there have been various updated versions with new norms. Incomplete sequences of diagrams are presented to subjects for completion and this requires the relationships between the diagrams to be worked out and the rule to be applied in selecting the correct answer. Such a process fits well with Spearman's definition and these matrices are the best loading test for fluid intelligence (Carroll, 1993). The only slight flaw is that the items are all of the same type so that specific variance can occasionally be troublesome – a few individuals are good at these items but not others.

The Mill–Hill and Crichton Scales (Raven, 1965b, 1965c)

These are two vocabulary tests to use alongside the matrices. As was discussed above, vocabulary is the best single measure of crystallised intelligence, so that a combination of one of these vocabulary tests and the Raven's matrices yields an excellent assessment of the two intelligence factors. Despite the age of these tests, they are still valuable in both research and in the applied field.

The Culture–Fair Test (Cattell and Cattell, 1959)

This is the test specifically designed by Cattell to measure fluid ability. It differs from Raven's in that there is a variety of items, in addition to matrices, in order to obviate problems of specific variance. All items are non-verbal, consisting of: analogies where the links between the first part of the analogy have to be worked out and applied to find the correct answer; series items (similar to matrices); classifications where the odd man out from a set of items has to be selected; matrices, as used in Raven's matrices; topological conditions, a special type of item in which, for example, from a set of diagrams one has to be chosen in which a dot could be placed between two circles but not in a square.

This Culture–Fair test is an excellent measure of fluid intelligence, as is to be expected from the types of items which all require the education of rules and their application to new cases.

Verbal Group Intelligence Tests

Finally I shall mention some well-known verbal intelligence tests which measure crystallised ability. These tests make use of analogies, classifications and series, just as the Culture–Fair test, but these are verbal. Because of this they require knowledge, vocabulary and a good understanding of English – hence the fact that they measure crystallised ability. Some good tests are the AH series of tests (which also have some non-verbal items) (Heim et al. 1970) which are good examples of verbal intelligence tests as is the Otis test (Otis, 1954).

Conclusions

In this chapter I have shown that the factor analysis of abilities has yielded two clear, correlated factors – fluid and crystallised intelligence which are largely heritable and account for much of the variance in human ability. These predict occupational and educational success and from the nature of their tests may be conceptualised as a general reasoning ability, crystallised intelligence resulting from the investment of fluid intelligence in the skills valued in a culture.

6
Personality Tests

Introduction

It was clear from Chapter 5 that in the field of intelligence and ability there was a considerable agreement both regarding what was to be measured (well-identified primary and secondary factors) and how these were to be measured. There is a remarkable similarity in the items used to measure human abilities. Furthermore it also became evident in this chapter that the measurement of ability is successful in that the tests have proved useful in applied psychology. As the most recent study showed (Schmidt and Hunter, 1998) the intelligence test is the best predictor of job success.

Unfortunately with personality testing all is different. There are many different kinds of personality tests, with little agreement between them. There is no real consensus as to what should be measured although there are claims concerning an agreed factor structure among personality questionnaires. This, however, is still a matter of dispute, as will be demonstrated. Furthermore, and perhaps worst of all, personality theories seem divorced from measurement. Finally, although widely used in applied psychology, personality tests are less powerful in prediction than tests of ability. All these problems and their possible resolution are the concern of this chapter.

Definition of Personality

Hall and Lindzey (1966) claimed that there are as many definitions of personality as there are theorists and this regrettably is the case. This makes measurement difficult since it is unclear where to begin. Furthermore many theories of personality, especially of the older type, use concepts which are not obviously quantitative. Jungian notions of archetypes and Freudian concepts such as the death and life instincts are of this kind. More modern approaches such as those of Murray or Maslow are open to similar objections. Furthermore since there is little evidence that any of these theories have a sound scientific basis it is arguable whether it makes sense to attempt to measure these variables at all. However, since, as has been argued, measurement is essential for science, it is important to define personality clearly as a basis for such measurement.

The Psychometric Solution to the Definition of Personality

Cattell (1957) adopted a solution to the problem of definition that essentially underpins most forms of personality measurement other than projective tests. Thus personality (or strictly temperament) is reflected in how we do what we do. Motivation, also an aspect of personality, refers to why we do what we do. For example, I might decide to tidy my room. How I do this reflects temperamental personality traits, such as conscientiousness and orderliness, and my reasons for so doing reflect dynamic traits such as fear of losing vital documents and annoyance at being unable to do simple tasks because of the mess. This is to conceive of personality as being defined in terms of position on various traits both dynamic and temperamental. The task of measurement therefore becomes clear. Tests must be developed to measure these traits. This, indeed, was the aim of Cattell and his colleagues to identify, through factor analysis, and measure the most important personality and motivational traits, together of course with abilities, and thus develop a quantified psychometric psychology. As I have previously argued (Kline, 1980) this is essentially to develop a psychometric model of human behaviour.

To achieve this Cattell (1957, for example) used two types of psychological test – personality questionnaires and objective tests, and these will be examined later in this chapter. Before I do this I shall begin our examination of personality testing by scrutinising a third category of personality test – projective tests.

Projective Tests

Projective tests, of which the two most famous examples are the Thematic Apperception Test, the TAT (Murray, 1971), and the Rorschach test (Rorschach, 1921), generally consist of ambiguous stimuli to which subjects have either to respond or which they describe. Some projective tests require the subject to complete sentences or to draw, as in the House Tree Person Test (Buck, 1948). There are several points about projective tests that need to be stressed and these are set out below.

- The meaning of projective. Projective tests are so called because it is assumed by their users that subjects respond to them by projecting their own conflicts and problems, often referred to as the deeper layers of personality. There are several important issues concerning personality measurement, implicit in this account of projections, and these are now set out.

- Ambiguity of the stimuli. The stimuli which subjects have to describe, for example symmetrical inkblots, in the case of the Rorschach, are ambiguous to encourage this projection, the assumption being that if clear stimuli are presented the stimulus itself would elicit the description. Thus unless subjects were deliberately lying, unable to see or psychotic, a perfectly accurate photograph of a banana would be simply thus described. However, although subjects must themselves supply a description of an object which cannot be recognised, it is only an assumption that such descriptions are projected from deep or unconscious layers of the personality.

- The meaning of projection. In Freudian theory there is a defence mechanism of projection. This, however, entails subjects denying painful or repugnant feelings by projecting these on to other people. Freud's most famous example of projection was that concerned with the delusions of persecution in paranoia which are claimed to arise from projection of hatred to their persecutors (Freud, 1911). However, there is little agreement concerning the scientific veracity of defences (Kline, 1981, Fisher and Greenberg, 1995) but even if there were, the projection of projective tests is quite different.

- No evidence for projection, as the term is used in projective tests. As Eysenck (1959) has argued, there is no evidence that subjects do project inner conflicts and feelings as is required by the rationale of projective tests. Thus it is clear that this aspect of the theoretical basis of projective tests is weak.

- The meaning of deeper layers of the personality. Again Eysenck (1996) has challenged the theoretical basis of projective tests. The terms shallow and deep are metaphors, if they mean anything at all, as is the notion of layers. In fact this is the metaphor underlying dynamic, psychoanalytic theories of personality. The id is conceived as a seething cauldron of desires kept down by the ego and superego, and it is these, presumably, which projective tests tap. However, the scientific validity of psychoanalytic theory has been questioned by many psychologists, especially Eysenck (1985) and more generally in terms of scientific method (Popper, 1959). Recently historical research has cast doubt on the truthfulness of Freud's own writing (Webster, 1995). I am not arguing here the case for or against Freud. However, it is clear that the concept of personality underlying projective tests is by no means agreed upon. Their theoretical basis is weak.

- Reliability of projective tests is low. The responses to projective tests have to be interpreted and scored. It has been shown again and again that the reliability of projective tests is low (Vernon, 1963).
- Validity of projective tests is low. Both Vernon (1963) and Eysenck (1959) have demonstrated that the validity of projective tests, especially the Rorschach test, is low. Indeed Eysenck claimed that the more rigorous the study the less valid projective tests appear to be. The reason for this is not simply the poor reliability of scoring the test. In addition Vernon (1963) showed that scores were affected by such variables as the sex of the tester, the race of the tester, the conditions of testing and what subjects thought that the test was about. For measures of the deeper layers of personality such criticisms are serious.
- Nomothetic vs idiographic measurement. Nomothetic measurement is concerned with the establishment of general rules or laws. Idiographic measurement, on the other hand, concentrates on the individual, the idiosyncratic. Projective tests in general are of this latter category. Allport (1937) argued that personality questionnaires, which are nomothetic, dealt with all that is common to individuals, whereas projective tests measured what is special to them and thus were of much greater psychological interest. While this may be true, in the sense that case studies are often fascinating, science demands that general laws be established. This distinction, idiographic compared with nomothetic tests, is important in our discussion below of why projective tests, despite these devastating criticism, are still used.

In Defence of Projective Tests

If it is accepted, as it must be, that projective tests have a weak theoretical basis, are unreliable, with low evidence of validity and are affected by trivial, extraneous variables, are there any grounds for using them? Below I briefly set out some of the counter arguments.

- Projective tests yield data which are quite different from that from other sources. Despite problems of reliability and validity the data of projective test responses are unique and thus deserve investigation.
- Projective test scores can be valuable. In the hands of experts some impressive personality research has been carried out with projective tests. Fine examples are the work of Murray (1938) in his development of personology, the study of the whole person, and Carstairs (1957) with his Rorschach studies of the Rajput. Of course tests which can

only be used by perhaps a few gifted individuals are not of great scientific value. Good measures should be reliable and valid for any user after training.

- Improving the scoring. It is possible to improve the reliability of scoring by specifying precisely how each response should be scored and by the study of such responses demonstrating their validity. Exner (1986) has done precisely this with the Rorschach. Entirely objective scoring is also possible, reducing the content of the responses to 1s and 0s. Holley (1973) has done this for the Rorschach and Hampson and Kline (1977) for some other projective tests in the study of criminals.

- Conclusions concerning projective tests. I agree with Eysenck that projective tests, scored in the traditional way, are not useful as scientific measures of personality. Interpretations are simply too easy. However, it is clear that they are good sources of data and with rigorous scoring and extensive empirical study of the psychological meaning of such scores they are worthy of investigation. However, it is to be hoped that truly scientific measures of personality with real units of measurement will be developed, as advocated in the New Psychometrics (Kline, 1998) and this would consign them to the dustbin of history, alongside all current psychometric tests.

Brief Descriptions of some Projective Tests

The Rorschach Test

Rorschach (1921) created this famous test consisting of ten symmetrical inkblots, half being monochrome in shades of grey, the others coloured or grey and coloured. Essentially subjects have to describe these blots and their responses are interpreted. As indicated, Exner (1986) has produced a detailed and reasonably objective scoring system but before this there were two complex and rival methods of scoring – those of Beck (1944) and Klopfer (Klopfer and Kelley, 1942). One problem with the Rorschach test is that it is claimed to be able to measure a huge variety of variables and this is *a priori* unlikely for any scientific measure. Furthermore, even given the scoring system of Exner, there is no unequivocal evidence of validity. However, it is worthy of quantitative investigation simply because of the apparent richness of the data.

The Thematic Apperception Test (TAT) (Murray, 1938)

This test consists of 31 stimuli, including a blank, each on a separate card. Subjects have to describe them. These cards show figures with ambiguous expressions and in ambiguous circumstances, for example a boy staring at a violin on a table and a boy clinging to a rope. Over the years variants of these cards have been produced for special purposes, such as cross-cultural testing, on the grounds that Murray (1938) argued that the essence of the tests was to provide stimulus for fantasy. Originally the cards were scored to assess the needs and presses (factors in the environment relevant to the needs) which are parts of Murray's account of personality. The need for achievement is perhaps the most famous of these. Over the years many other different scoring schemes have been developed (for example, Karon, 1981). In general there is not much empirical support for the validity of the TAT although in Murray's hands it yielded highly interesting information. Since the cards are now old-fashioned (subjects think that they are pictures of old films) and since the author admitted that other stimuli could be as effective, I believe this test should be consigned to an honourable retirement.

House Tree Person Test (Buck, 1948)

In this test subjects are required to draw a house, a tree and a person. They are then asked questions about their drawings and all the results are then interpreted according to the test manual which has been updated (Buck, 1970). One feature of this test is that it can be scored objectively with good reliability. However, the interpretations, offered in the manual, fit Eysenck's (1959) notorious description of projective tests reflecting the riotous imaginations of clinicians. For example, it is claimed that a small chimney or no chimney is evidence of castration complex and shuttered windows are held to reflect a person who resists advances, interpretations based on metaphor, although supported sometimes by case studies. This is an interesting test which yields rich data and it deserves investigation using rigorous objective methods but its current interpretations could not be treated seriously.

Objective Tests

The second category of personality tests and the least used is that of objective tests, sometimes referred to as performance tests (for example, Cronbach, 1984). Cattell (1957) is the main exponent of the use of objective tests and Cattell and Warburton (1967) have published a compendium of all such tests available at that time which included 688 tests from which more than 2000 variables were derived. This is still the standard source for objective personality tests and it is their definition and approach which are the basis of this discussion.

- Definition of an objective test. An objective test is one which can be objectively scored and (crucially) one of which the purpose is hidden from subjects. In addition it must be a task which produces some variance. Thus the construction of such tests is not difficult although demonstrating what they measure and designing them deliberately to measure a variable is no simple task (see Cattell and Warburton, 1967 and Kline, 1999 for a discussion of this difficulty).

- Advantages of objective personality testing. Because subjects are unable to guess what is being measured, deliberate cheating and distortion, both of which are problems in applied testing, especially in selection, are minimised if not eliminated. In addition, problems typical of questionnaires, such as social desirability, the tendency to endorse a response because it is socially desirable so to do, and acquiescence, the tendency to agree with an item regardless of content, are usually eliminated. Finally because, as shall be seen, objective tests need not require language, other than understanding what to do, they could be useful in cross-cultural psychology.

- Problems with objective tests: principles of construction. Despite these advantages there are problems with objective tests, of which one has been mentioned. In our definition of these tests it was argued that any task which yielded variance and which could be objectively scored was an objective test. However, given so broad a definition, principles for designing such tests ought to be available. Cattell and Warburton (1967) in fact discuss some principles at great length but are forced to conclude that their somewhat abstract system in practice may not be that useful. A definite problem lies in the fact that objective tests could, in principle, measure ability, personality or motivation and, as has been argued, a test which measured any combination of these variables would not be useful. The best approach to objective test construction is to attempt to derive tests from psychological theories and observations and in some clinical instances this might be possible. For example, obsessionals dislike their hands being dirty. Thus a situation could be set up in which subjects have a horrible substance spilled on their hands. Their responses could be noted: length of time they spend cleaning it off; what they say to the tester; heart rate when the spillage is first observed. That the construction of valid tests is difficult is attested by the fact that very few of the tests in the Compendium (an indexed classification of proposed objective tests of personality) have any evidence for validity.

- Validating objective tests. As has been argued, constructing objective tests *per se* is not difficult. What is hard is constructing such tests to measure a particular variable. Thus one approach to obtaining a set of valid objective tests would be to factor a large number of objective tests together with marker tests for the best established personality and ability factors. An examination of such factor matrices would establish clearly objective tests which overlapped these criterion, marker factors, and objective tests which measured clear factors which were different from the markers. These would need independent external validation. It would also show if objective tests were mixtures of personality and ability and, therefore, not useful for measurement. However, this is a huge task which has really not been attempted except with a few selected tests.

Conclusions Concerning Objective Tests

The great advantage of objective tests, that they are opaque in meaning, is offset by the fact that few have evidence of validity and given the problems of their rationale, clear evidence of validity is essential.

In the remainder of this section, I shall list and briefly describe some objective tests, selected from the Compendium to illustrate their ingenuity and diversity, including those which Cattell regards as the most valid and which have been published as personality tests. For more details see Kline (1999), Hundleby (1973) and Cattell and Warburton (1967).

Some Examples of Objective Tests

- The fidgetometer. This a chair with electrical contacts in the arms and seat. It thus measures how much a subject fidgets, in a given situation. It is not detectable and if it were it would be difficult to know how best to score. It was assumed that high scores would load the anxiety factor but this was not so. Thus the fidgetometer fully exemplifies objective test construction: a clever rationale, great ingenuity and yet no validity.
- Slow line drawing. Subjects are required to draw a line as slowly as possible on a page in a given time. Several objective indices are scored: the length of the line; whether the subject cheated (by lifting the pencil or by stopping). Again, however, the factor loadings on this test did not conform with expectation, for example loading on inhibition and a cheating factor (psychoticism, discussed in our next section on personality questionnaires).
- Shock suggestibility. Subjects are hooked up to an apparatus which they are informed gives them a mild shock. They are told to move a dial which increases the shock to the point when they can just feel it. Various scores can be obtained including the average point on the dial at which the subject reports a shock, and a report of no shock. There is no current. This test loads a timidity factor.

- Dark adaptation. This is a test in which subjects are required, in darkness, to look at a bright screen for 30 seconds. This is then turned off and the time taken until they can report a letter on the screen is noted. This loads the inhibition factor in objective tests.

- Other objective tests. These examples from the Compendium illustrate some of the ingenuity which has gone into objective test construction. Many types of objective tests are, or more strictly appear to be, more conventional and I shall give a few examples, although a proper sample is impossible in this Primer. One is a questionnaire in which subjects have to rate on a five-point scale how good some performance is, for example learning to skate in two lessons. The objective score is the number of extremes. In objective tests acquiescence is actually used as a score, rather than being regarded as a response set, to be eliminated, when a questionnaire is given. In another test pairs of book titles are given and subjects state preferences. The score for this particular test is the ratio of the number of socially acceptable titles chosen to the number of socially unacceptable titles chosen. This is an example of a social desirability response tendency being indexed as an objective test score.

- Some published objective tests. From the huge number of tests in the Compendium Cattell and his colleagues collected some of the best validated examples and published them as complete tests. Kline (1999) has described these in detail and examined their validity and reliability but some brief comments here will be useful.

- The Objective Analytic Test Battery (OATB) (Cattell and Schuerger, 1978). This consists of 70 objective tests purportedly measuring ten factors: self-assertion; independence; evasiveness; exuberance; emotional balance; anxiety; realism; self-assurance; extraversion and pessimism. These factors, as was always the case with the work of Cattell, were extracted from simple structure rotations. However, because these tests were so unusual and potentially valuable in the study of personality, Kline and Cooper (1984b) carried out two factor analyses of these tests, reaching simple structure by the methods discussed in Chapter 4. Unfortunately the results of these investigations did not support the validity of the test. To identify the factors the OATB factors were factor analysed together with the EPQ and 16PF personality questionnaire factors (described in the next section of this chapter), the best established ability factors (as described in Chapter 5) and some measure of the authoritarian personality (Adorno et al., 1950). The OATB factors did not emerge. Furthermore, many of the factors were often mixtures of personality and ability. It had to be concluded that the OATB was not a valid test and that most of the factors were not factor-pure.

- The Motivation Analysis Test (MAT) (Cattell et al., 1970b). This test claims to measure the dynamic aspects of personality, hence its title. It measures two sets of variables – ergs (basic drives) – and sentiments (culturally moulded drives). Within these sets two aspects can be measured – integrated and unintegrated components which are roughly equivalent to conscious and unconscious (Cattell and Child, 1975). I have subjected this test to careful examination because, as is discussed in Chapter 7, motivation tests are somewhat weak and the MAT, if valid, would be a powerful instrument having been developed through wide-ranging factor analyses of motivational variables (Cattell and Child, 1975). Kline and Grindley (1974) carried out a 28-day case study of the MAT in which daily fluctuations of the test scores appeared to be related to the events in a subject's life, as recorded in a diary. However, psychometric examination of the MAT by Cooper and Kline (1982) showed that the scale was not valid, at least in the UK. A simple structure rotation of the MAT and the 16PF test failed to yield the ten scales, the eight factors emerging making no obvious sense. Furthermore item analysis of the scales (see Chapter 4) showed that the scales were not homogeneous. Items did not fit their scales.

Objective Tests: Finale

It must be concluded that, at present, objective personality tests are not suitable for use, other than to investigate their validity. If all the tests in the Compendium were subjected to rigorous, psychometric research a small number of useful and valid tests might emerge. But this is a huge task and there are few investigators in this field. It is probably more useful to attempt to develop better theories of personality and motivation as an aid to constructing such tests. Good theorising is better than pure empiricism.

Personality Questionnaires

Personality questionnaires or inventories (I shall use these terms interchangeably) consist of questions or statements relevant to a subject's behaviour to which the subject responds. 'Do you sleep well?' and 'I dislike films with a strong love interest' are typical items. Personality inventories are widely used in applied psychology of all kinds, particularly in selection.

Advantages of Personality Questionnaires

Compared with objective and projective tests there are clear advantages in favour of personality questionnaires and the most important of these are set out below.

- Group administration. Personality questionnaires can be administered to subjects in groups. When large numbers of people have to be tested this is a great advantage since projective tests, generally, have to be administered individually, as do some objective tests.
- Ease of scoring. Scoring is entirely objective and requires no skill. Personality questionnaires can be presented on computer (see Chapter 8) and these are scored automatically. This contrasts with the laborious scoring of projective tests and many objective tests. The use of projective tests (including interpretation) requires considerable training.
- Reliability and validity of personality questionnaires. As has been discussed many projective tests are not reliable and have poor evidence of validity and this latter is true of objective tests. However, personality inventories, since they consist of sets of items, can be constructed according to the principles described in Chapter 4. This means that it is easy to construct a highly reliable (in the sense of both test–retest and internal consistency) personality inventory. Furthermore it is easy to collect good norms, although the demonstration of validity, as with all tests, is not a simple matter. Nevertheless, it is the case that there is a small number of personality tests of high reliability and with good evidence for validity, although there is less agreement in the field of personality measurement than with tests of ability. Such tests will be briefly described later in this section.

Problems with Personality Questionnaires

Since these tests can be reliable, valid and well standardised and, in addition, are simple to administer, an obvious question arises – why do researchers bother with other types of personality test? In fact many do not. In the applied field questionnaires rule, although incredibly graphology is used, despite the fact that its validity is known to be zero (for example, Kanfer et al., 1995). However, there are some problems with personality inventories which are often conveniently ignored. Again these are briefly set out below.

- Meaning of items. Heim (1975) argued that the items of personality tests were so absurd that it was insulting to ask subjects to complete such tests and that items of such banality could not embrace anything important about human behaviour. This is the converse of the argument in favour of projective tests – the richness of their data. There is force to this claim by Heim. A summary of some memorable items which are by no means rare easily makes the case: would you drink blood? Is your heart beating in the morning? Would you prefer to go round a bank or a sewage farm? Do you often feel miserable for no particular reason? In brief, items are so simple that it seems somewhat incredible that they could measure much of importance. However, there are other problems with items.

- Face validity. These items supposedly reflect behaviour. That is the assumption. But is this the case? There are known problems affecting responses to items which mean that their face validity should not be taken on trust. These include: response sets of acquiescence and social desirability; deliberate lying (obviously a problem in selection); simple delusion and false belief about one's nature; lack of information about others making the use of terms such as 'frequently' and 'usually' difficult. Personality test items are not samples of the behaviour we are trying to test, only reports about such behaviour and this alone differentiates them from ability test items.

- Meaning of factors. This is a related problem to that of face validity. Personality test items are chosen by selecting items loading a particular factor. However, such factors can be simply semantic – that is factors consisting of items whose correlation is entailed by their meaning. This implies that all personality factors must be externally validated. Factors cannot be identified simply from the meaning of the items loading their factors. As has been demonstrated in detail by Kline (1999) this is not always done. Often test constructors feel they have done enough by demonstrating that their tests are loading common factors.

Conclusions Concerning the Value of Personality Questionnaires

Personality questionnaires can be made reliable and with good norms. These are essential characteristics for good measurement. In addition they are convenient to administer and score. However, it is far too easy to construct reliable item sets which are simply bloated specifics and thus only tests of which the validity has been clearly demonstrated should be used other than for investigations of test validity. In fact there are a few such tests and these together with the rationale for their selection and a discussion of the evidence for validity will be set out below.

The Validity of Personality Questionnaires

As was discussed in the opening section of this chapter, a problem with the measurement of personality resides in the lack of agreement among personality theories and the consequent problems of knowing what is to be measured. Cattell (1957) and Eysenck (1967a), to cite the most salient of their huge output relevant to this discussion, have attempted to overcome this difficulty through a combination of factor analysis and experimental psychology, two approaches which have been long divorced with grievous consequences. Both Eysenck and Cattell have stressed the importance of developing factors which have an external basis for validation in experimental psychology, biology, genetics or other external criteria. Thus the mere emergence of factors from a set of items is not sufficient.

In the discussion below I set out the personality factors which meet these criteria. These factors can be reliably found in the analysis of personality questionnaires, just as the ability factors in Chapter 5 were found in the analysis of ability tests. In addition these personality factors are embedded in psychological theory. I shall also, finally, briefly describe the personality questionnaires which measure these factors.

Personality Factors

In the field of personality inventories, many workers have developed tests through factor analysis and many have claimed that their set of factors best describes the field. As I write there is a consensus that five factors best describe the field of personality, a finding which is referred to as the five-factor model or the big five and its main proponents are Costa and McCrae (for example, 1992b). However, it is noteworthy that Cattell (Boyle et al., 1995) has powerful arguments against this model as has Eysenck (1992), arguments which appear to me to be difficult to refute as I have shown in detail (Kline, 1998, 1999). Because of this current consensus, it is necessary to describe this model and to point out its difficulties, before setting out a more acceptable solution.

The Five-Factor Model

As the name suggests, five second-order factors are claimed in this model to account for much of the variance in personality questionnaires. Costa and McCrae (1992b) argue that these factors can also be found on re-analysis of the majority of personality questionnaires including the Gough Adjective Check List (Piedmont et al., 1991), the MMPI (Costa et al., 1985), the Personality Research Form (Costa and McCrae, 1988), and the Myers–Briggs (McCrae and Costa, 1989). Well-known researchers in this field endorse this view, for example, Digman (1990), Pervin (1990) and Goldberg (1992). These factors are set out below.

- Extraversion. The extravert is sociable and hungry for stimulation. The introvert, the low scorer, is quiet, reflective and withdrawn.
- Anxiety. This is the well-known factor of trait anxiety. Low scorers are stolid, unemotional and unflappable. The high scorer is excitable, moody, and worries a lot.

- Agreeableness. The high scorer is likeable and fits in well with others in contrast to her opposite at the low pole.
- Conscientiousness. The higher scorer is reliable, obeys rules, and does everything as well as possible, again in contrast to the low scorer.
- Openness. The high scorer is open to new ideas, flexible, liberal in contrast to the rigid conservatism of those with a closed mind.

Arguments Against the Five-Factor Model

As I have stated above, I cannot accept this model for a number of reasons.

- O, A, and C are not independent. These factors are correlated as Boyle et al. (1995) point out. This suggests that there is an imperfect approach to simple structure and that these factors are the result of poor measurement. Draycott and Kline (1995) investigated precisely this point in a study of the EPQ (Eysenck and Eysenck, 1975), the best measure of extraversion and anxiety (see below) and the NEO which is McCrae and Costa's measure of the five factors. They found that P (Eysenck's tough-minded factor) loaded the same cannonical variate as C, A and O which confirmed their lack of independence and their relationship to P, as Eysenck has argued (Eysenck, 1992).
- The meaning of O, A and C. As has been demonstrated, with personality factors it is insufficient to label factors from the nature of items loading the factors. Thus it is necessary to ask what is the psychological meaning of these factors. Whereas extraversion and anxiety have a physiological basis (Eysenck, 1967a) and are aspects of many psychological theories, the abstraction of conscientiousness, agreeablesness and openness is arbitrary.
- The five-factor solution is far from simple structure. As has been argued the correlations between the last three factors suggest that simple structure has not been reached and this is confirmed by examination of the low loadings in the factor matrix. This is serious, as was shown in Chapter 4, since where there is no simple structure there is no reason to accept a factor analytic solution, which is simply one of an infinity. Costa and McCrae (1992b) have attempted to argue that simple structure is not important and that personality traits are not necessarily unifactorial. However, for reasons which have been made clear, this will not do.
- Conclusions. On all these grounds, which have been fully endorsed by Block (1995), it would appear that, despite the consensus, it is contrary to the evidence to regard these five factors as best accounting for the variance in personality questionnaires.

The Work of Cattell

One of the truly great psychometrists, Cattell, over a period of 60 years, published copiously in the factor analysis of personality, motivation and abilities and was a pioneer in all these areas. He realised that the successful exploratory analysis of personality depended on a proper sampling of the field and this he attempted by his notion of the semantic personality sphere. He argued that if traits existed there must be words for them. He, therefore, from a dictionary search of descriptive terms for behaviour and the elimination of synonyms finally emerged with a core of traits for which ratings were developed. From analyses of these ratings 12 factors emerged (L factors). He then developed questionnaires to measure these factors – the 16PF Questionnaire – 16 because four questionnaire factors were discovered (Cattell et al., 1970a). This test has received continuous development and is still in use today. These 16 factors, which Cattell argued formed the basic structure of personality, were extensively studied by Cattell and colleagues in work reported in many books and papers and summarised in Cattell (1973) and Cattell and Kline (1977). The theoretical side was explicated in Cattell (1981).

The development of these factors through life, their environmental and genetic determinants, were set out as well as their correlations with real life behaviour, success in jobs, academic success and clinical outcomes. It formed a brilliant psychometric account of human behaviour.

Problems with the 16 Factors

Cattell began work on personality in the 1940s before powerful computers were available and the 16-factor structure which first emerged is probably not the best solution. Many later investigators have failed to find these factors (for example, Howarth 1976) which Cattell attributed to shortcomings in the factor analyses. However, Kline and Barrett (1983), in a detailed study of personality questionnaires including the 16PF, followed the technical minutiae to the letter and still failed to recover the primary 16 factors. Among the reasons for this failure were the following.

- The reliabilities of the 16PF scales are low. This adds in error.
- A study of the original basis of the Cattell factors indicated that Cattell accepted items with low loadings as satisfactory when most investigators would have rejected them.
- Conclusions. For these reasons the primary factors of Cattell could not be regarded as a satisfactory account of personality structure, despite the brilliance and the magnitude of Cattell's research programme.

- The second-order factors. Although the 16 primary factors could not be recovered second-order analysis revealed four stable factors: extraversion; anxiety; tough-mindedness; and conventionality. Two comments are useful here. These are clearly similar to the factors of the five-factor model and two of them, anxiety and extraversion, correlated highly with their counterparts in the EPQ. Krug and Johns (1986) recovered similar secondary factors from a huge study of more than 17 000 subjects.
- Conclusions concerning the Cattell factors. The primaries are clearly not as Cattell claimed but the second-order factors are similar to those in the five-factor model. However, caution has to be shown since the primaries on which they are based are difficult to interpret.

The Work of Eysenck

Eysenck, along with Cattell, has contributed hugely to the understanding of personality combining factor analysis and experimental psychology in a huge output of books and papers. It is this combination which ensures that his factors measured by the EPQ (Eysenck and Eysenck, 1975) and its revision, the EPQ-R (Eysenck and Eysenck, 1995), are far more than collections of semantically similar items. His factors are grounded in physiology and in conditioning theory and their genetic determinants have been examined (Eaves et al., 1989). Furthermore, these factors have been implicated by Eysenck and his colleagues in a huge array of different human behaviour – smoking, neurosis and psychosis, criminality, differential performance in jobs and road accidents, to name but a few. Some of this work is summarised conveniently in Modgil and Modgil (1986).

The three factors which Eysenck (1967a, 1992) considers best to account for variance in personality are set out below.

- Extraversion (E). As described previously the extravert is sociable, lively and in terms of Eysenck's theory stimulus hungry.
- Neuroticism (N). Eysenck calls his second factor neuroticism since he regards this as basic to neurosis although empirically it is certainly identical to the factor labelled anxiety in the work previously discussed. This factor is trait anxiety.
- Psychoticism (P). This is the somewhat exotic label given to a factor in which high scorers are cruel, hard, ruthless and entirely lacking in empathy. They like risk taking and danger and this factor is related to criminality and is generally lower in females.

Comments on these Three Factors

Two of these factors are similar to those of the five-factor model and the second order in the Cattell system. However, the Eysenck factors are not simply collections of items which load a factor, for the following reasons.

- Heritability. If these were simply semantic factors their heritability would not be high (around .5) as it has been shown to be by Eaves et al. (1989).
- Physiological bases. Extraversion has been claimed to be a function of the arousability of the central nervous system, while neuroticism is regarded as related to the lability of the autonomic nervous system. Psychoticism is more tentatively held to be correlated with androgen production. Evidence for this springs from studies of the EEG (Stelmack and Houlihan, 1995) and from work on conditioning extraverts and introverts (Eysenck, 1967a), although Fahrenberg (1992) has called into question the whole notion of arousability.
- Replicability of these factors. Kline and Barrett (1983) showed that N and E items loaded their factors almost perfectly although there were problems with P mainly because normals score low on this factor. Such results are generally agreed by almost all factor analysts (Mathews and Deary, 1998).

Conclusions Concerning the Factor Structure of Personality

Without question two personality factors can be reliably found in personality questionnaires and these make, as Eysenck has shown, considerable psychological sense. These are extraversion and neuroticsm or anxiety. For these there is a benchmark marker test – the EPQ (Eysenck and Eysenck, 1975). As regards the other second-order factors it seems possible that the confusion can be resolved by adding a third factor of obsessional personality. The obsessional personality is rule-bound, careful, rigid, conscientious, dogmatic and inflexible. This description embraces aspects of P, psychoticism; O, openness; C, conscientiousness; and A, agreeableness. It fits theoretical accounts of dogmatism (Rokeach, 1960), the anal character (Freud, 1908), and the authoritarian personality (Adorno et al., 1950). Furthermore such a second order was supported by a factor analytic study of a variety of measures of authoritarian personality by Kline and Cooper (1984c). It may well be that P, as Eysenck suggests, is fundamental to this factor and further work will resolve this question.

Some Important Personality Questionnaires

To complete this chapter I shall simply list and make some brief comments upon the most commonly used personality questionnaires. However, a detailed analysis of many personality questionnaires can be found in Kline (1999) and Bartram et al. (1995).

The Eysenck Personality Questionnaire (Eysenck and Eysenck, 1975)

This is the standard test for the three factors discussed above, E, N and P. It is highly reliable and with good evidence of validity. It has 90 items including a lie scale to attempt to filter out those attempting to present themselves in a good light. There is a junior version for children.

The Cattell Personality Questionnaires (the 16PF)

There are several versions of these tests – parallel forms for adults, high school, junior school and pre-school versions for developmental studies. The most recent adult form is that of Conn and Riecke (1994) but this is so changed from the original that the huge body of research on the 16PF scales may not be applicable. As has been argued, the original scales had low reliabilities and the factor structure was difficult to replicate. On the other hand, there was so much research relevant to the scales that their psychological meaning was rich. There are extensive norms for American occupations and this test is still widely used in occupational selection both in this country and in America.

NEO-PI-R (Costa and McCrae, (1992a)

This is the newest version of the test on which the five-factor model of personality is based. It measures the five factors – neuroticism, extraversion, openness, conscientiousness and agreeableness with good reliability (all scales >.7). In addition it breaks down each factor into a number of facets, for example anger and depression for neuroticism and competence and order for C. However, these facets are measured by only eight items. The value of this test depends upon the evaluation of the five-factor model.

These are the tests which measure the factors which must be considered as among the best accounts of the structure of personality. Nevertheless there are some other tests which are widely used and these will be briefly mentioned although for full evaluations readers must refer to Kline (1999) and Bartram et al. (1995).

The MMPI (MMPI-2, Butcher, 1990, is the Latest Version)

The original Minnesota Multiphasic Personality Questionnaire was one of the most widely used personality questionnaires, although its validity and reliability have been regularly called into question (Graham, 1990). This test was constructed by the criterion-keyed method (see Chapter 4) and was first used among clinical groups, but many other scales have been developed by similar methods from its large number of items. Factoring this test makes it clear that it is essentially a measure of N and there is little evidence of the validity of any of the other scales. Its clinical popularity is difficult to support in the light of such a report and it is likely that the new version is highly similar.

Some Other Tests

Well-known tests are the Californian Psychological Inventory (Gough and Cook, 1997) which has been called the sane man's MMPI and was developed by similar procedures, and finally a set of tests developed commercially by the testing firm Saville and Holdworth. These are the Occupational Personality Questionnaires of which there are many different versions, some developed by factor analysis and some ipsative. These are widely used in selection and have been found useful by practitioners although they do not factor exactly as claimed by their authors (Barrett et al., 1996).

Summary

- Projective tests, if they are to be used for their rich data, require objective methods of scoring which require validation.
- Objective tests, despite their advantages, need a sound theoretical basis and, again, good evidence for validity, before they can be used.
- Personality questionnaires can be made homogeneous and reliable but items are only reports of behaviour and the meaning of factors requires validation.
- The five-factor model is not as definitive as is sometimes claimed. Clearly anxiety and extraversion are regularly found in questionnaires. Obsessional characteristics in some form appear to emerge as a factor, as does psychoticism.
- All personality factors need to be validated against external criteria and tied into a proper theory of personality.

7
Motivation, Mood, Attitude and Other Tests

In this chapter I shall discuss a variety of tests which do not fall into the categories of personality or ability. It will not be possible to examine in any detail tests for specialised purposes as might be used in clinical psychology, or tests of defences which are dynamic concepts, but I shall deal with tests designed to measure motivation, the dynamics of behaviour. These are variously called tests of states (as distinct from traits), moods, and even interests.

I shall also say something about the measurement of attitudes, which are obviously an important aspect of social psychology, although, as it happens, there are relatively few published attitude scales. Generally investigators construct their own tests specifically tailored for their purposes, and thus the methods of attitude measurement must be scrutinised.

Some readers may well have heard of computerised tests and these will clearly become of greater significance as the influence of computers becomes yet greater. These, however, I shall discuss in Chapter 8, since their use is very much part of applied psychology.

The Meaning of Motivation

In Chapter 6 we saw that one of the problems in the measurement of personality was the vagueness of the concept which made it difficult to know what variables to measure. As was hinted there, this is an even greater difficulty in the measurement of motivation. This is partly because the factor analysis of motivation is far less developed than is the case with personality and there is nothing approaching consensus, except possibly in the study of moods. This lack of factor analysis stems from the weakness of motivational theories and concepts.

Terminology

Motivation refers to the dynamics of behaviour. It refers to our motives, our reasons for doing what we do. Because there is no clear accepted theory of human behaviour, many different dynamic terms are used and these form the variables of motivational measures. However, these terms require clarification since they are often essentially synonymous.

States

Some dynamic variables are referred to as states. The clearest example is anxiety. State anxiety refers to the anxiety induced by some event, for example an impending exam or a medical diagnosis. These raise anxiety in the majority of individuals. If the diagnosis is benign, there is a sudden reduction of the anxiety state. Thus states fluctuate. This is in contrast to traits. Trait anxiety is our average level, independent of particular events and it does not change. This is the distinction between traits and states. The former are static, the latter fluctuate with our experiences. While state and trait anxiety are commonsensical notions, Cattell (1973) has claimed that other traits have associated states, although the evidence for this is less convincing. However, in conclusion, states are one class of dynamic variable that require measurement and state anxiety can be measured, as will be seen below.

Moods

Moods are another dynamic concept which is part of everyday psychology. We do things because we are angry or tired, for example. The number of moods which come immediately to mind is large: anger, fear, fatigue, sadness, joy, cheerfulness and so on. This suggests that factor analysis might be useful to elucidate their structure and this has been employed with some success. The findings from such analyses will be discussed in our section on the measurement of moods as will the problems of such measurement. But a few points need to be made here.

Difference between moods and states   Cattell (1973) suggests that there is no true difference between these terms. Of course there are some distinctions in their use in English but these are linguistic conventions rather than indicators of a real conceptual distinction. As with states, moods fluctuate. Few people remain enraged continuously, for example. If we compare anger and state anxiety, they seem little different in kind. Both fluctuate; both are excited by experiences and damped down by them; both appear to drive behaviour, and this is true of almost all moods and states.

Duration of moods   Some moods are very brief. It is difficult, for example, to feel elation for long but sadness can last and in clinical cases may be virtually as stable as a trait. This exemplifies the fact that generally the term mood is used for brief states and states for longer lasting ones. Sometimes, as in the case of sadness, the state resembles a trait. This is important because it could be the case that the distinction between state and trait is arbitrary and does not reflect actual psychology. Clearly this is a matter of empirical research. There is a further salient point, namely the possibility that some moods are so brief that they cannot be measured by a conventional test.

Drives

Some theorists of motivation, notably McDougall (1932) and Murray (1938), discuss motivation in terms of drives. In this work drives are thought to be biological in origin. Hunger, thirst and sex are obvious drives of this type which are also part of the vernacular approach to motivation. One feature of such drives, and this makes them attractive for a scientific approach, is that they may be found among other mammals. This is important because *Homo sapiens* is simply a species of mammal and its genetic make-up must be shared amongst mammals. Certainly, it is accepted that hunger and sexual drives determine behaviour. However, before the measurement of such drives can be understood there are several points about the concept of drive which must be briefly examined.

Circularity of the arguments for drives   It is sometimes argued that aggressive actions are caused by an individual having a high level of aggression or aggressive drive. However, the evidence for this aggressive drive is the aggressive action which it is supposed to determine. On such a basis one could say that all actions are caused by corresponding drives and propensities, which, indeed, is precisely what McDougall (1932) did argue. This line of argument is flawed. If one posits drives then they must be supported by evidence independent of the behaviour which they are supposed to drive. For example, it could be argued that there was an aggressive drive which resulted from the amount of testosterone circulating at any given time. This is not circular and is a testable proposition.

Biology and culture   Of course few would deny that hunger and thirst are drives of a biological origin although there are cultural factors on how these are satisfied. However, many would argue that, in addition, there are drives which are culturally moulded, and the desire for money is taken as an obvious example (Cattell and Child, 1975). Such drives are referred to as sentiments by McDougal (1932) and Cattell and Child (1975). In other words some drives are products of our culture rather than our biology. This may be correct but it could be argued, it should be noted, that sentiments may be cultural forms of expressing biological drives. Thus, in Japan, hunger is assuaged by raw fish while in Great Britain we prefer it battered (or we did until health faddists and the Islington Socialists ruined our diets). Similarly, it may be that the desire for money is the cultural form of demonstrating status as the alpha ape. This leads on to a third point.

Problems with broad or general theories of motivation   Some authors have suggested that behaviour is driven by a few broad instincts or drives. However, such accounts are notoriously difficult to test because they are so flexible that little cannot be fitted to them. Freud (1923), for example, argued that there was a conflict of two drives – eros, the desire to live, and thanatos, the desire to return whence we came. Another example is the claim that all organisms are driven simply by the desire to replicate, often referred to as the Selfish Gene theory (Dawkins, 1976) although the notion is not his but comes from sociobiology. This one higher-order factor, if correct, would have to be shown to load on other basic drives. However, this necessitates that these be measured. A psychologically powerful account of motivation would have to be able to test such theorising since it appears to fit well with non-human species.

Interests

This is the last term which I shall discuss before scrutinising the psychometric studies of motivation. Psychologists working in the applied field of industrial psychology are often concerned with motivation on the commonsense ground, which may be tautological, that well-motivated workers are better than their opposites. For these psychologists the term interest is often used and there is a variety of interest tests, the assumption being that interests motivate individuals, for example entomologists are entomologists because they are interested in butterflies. However, the notion of interests may be an example of a redundant concept. Thus an interest in x is inferred if a subject spends time and effort working at x. It is then claimed that an interest in x causes the subject to work at x although the only evidence of such an interest is the fact that the subject works at x. This is a similar argument to the one used against the notion of drives. The concept is vacuous unless some independent evidence can be adduced for it. While this might be possible in the case of drives, as has been argued, for interests there seem greater difficulties. However, this has not deterred psychometric test developers and there are many tests of interests.

Reinforcement

The notion of motivation is particularly anathema to the behaviourist (for example, Skinner, 1953) because in this approach to understanding human behaviour, internal subjective states, which can never be publicly observed, cannot be part of science. Furthermore it is argued that behaviour is determined by reinforcement. Thus what is required is the study of reinforcers not unobservable moods, states, drives, sentiments, instincts or interests. Of course behaviourists would object to all trait psychology but motivation is particularly antithetical because reinforcers are considered to maintain behaviour, in direct opposition to motivational traits.

Conclusions Concerning the Terminology of Motivation

I have examined carefully the meanings of the terms used in the study of motivation. It is obvious that the field is conceptually confused and that the epistemic status of many of the concepts is dubious. States and moods are only different by linguistic convention and the notion of drive is essentially biological although drives require to be identified on grounds other than the behaviour which they are supposed to drive, and the same is true of sentiments and interests. Over all these terms hangs the spectre of redundancy, stemming from the concept of reinforcement. Thus when it comes to the study of tests of motivation, it will only be for the sake of convenience that I shall deal separately with moods, states, drives and interests.

The Factor Analysis of Motivation

From our discussion above it is obvious that motivation is not so clearly understood that there can be no question as to what variables should be measured. In this it resembles the field of personality. Actually this understates the real position. There is almost no agreement as to what should be measured or how this should be done.

In a complex field such as this, with no guidelines as to the critical variables, exploratory analysis would appear to be ideal and Cattell and colleagues have, as might be expected, attempted this solution to the problems of measurement (Cattell and Child, 1975). However, this is almost the sole attempt and there is no doubt that Cattell's work on motivation is less developed than in the fields of personality and ability. One of the reasons for this lies in the difficulty of deciding what variables could be called motivational in the first place, an essential in a factor analysis. However, in addition to this, there are problems specific to the factor analysis of motivation and these must be discussed.

- Dynamic variables change over time. As we have seen, states and moods change over time and this is what distinguishes them from traits. The same is true of drives as they are sated or not or as physiology changes. Thus, as Cattell (1973) argues, to be sure that factors are dynamic the factor analysis must involve time, in some way. If it does not there can be no certainty that the factors are dynamic: they may be traits.

- Time in factor analysis.
- The regular R factor analysis of variables leads to traits which account for differences between people. Traits can emerge only from R analysis.
- P factor analysis requires that one individual is tested many times on each variable. The factors emerging from the correlations between the variables are dynamic but are unique to that individual. This is time-consuming and few individuals could be assembled who would submit to such testing. Furthermore constant retesting is likely to destroy the validity of tests. Finally, as has been mentioned, some states are short-lived and thus retesting would be impossible. For all these reasons, P factor analysis has been rarely used. Cattell (1973) and Cattell and Kline (1977) have suggested two further methods which are practicable and still involve time.
- dR factor analysis. This involves the factor analysis of the differences between the scores of subjects on two occasions. The resulting factors must be dynamic – moods or states. Cronbach (1976) claims that difference scores are unreliable and this would lower the reliability of the factor analyses. One way round this is to use large samples and split them in order to replicate the dR analyses. Only replicated factors would be interpreted. However, a recent paper by Zimmerman and Williams (1998) has demonstrated that in many testing contexts the reliability of difference scores is not much reduced.
- Chain P analysis. This combines dR and P analysis. Thus if ten subjects are tested on 5 occasions, it is possible to analyse the data as if there were 50 occasions.
- Conclusions. From these arguments the following conclusions may be drawn which strongly affect how the research which is discussed below is interpreted.

  - Traits can appear only in R analysis.
  - States can appear in R, dR and P analysis.
  - Change factors (which will be discussed below) can appear in dR and P analysis.
  - Thus by studying where factors appear in all three analyses their proper status can be worked out.

Results from the Psychometric Analysis of Motivation

We are now in a position to evaluate the psychometric measurement of motivation. I shall begin with moods and states.

The Factor Analysis of States

The work of Cattell is described in three publications: Cattell (1973), Cattell and Kline (1977) and Cattell and Child (1975). In this Primer I can only summarise what is a field of great complexity. We have seen how states are distinguished from traits on the grounds of transience. This means that to be certain a factor is a state or mood it must be found in dR or P analysis. However, when Cattell (1973) applied dR analysis he discovered that there were many more factors than he had anticipated. For example, most of the trait factors appeared in dR analysis. However, Cattell (1973) argued that these were not true state factors. These were change factors. These factors make no sense as states but reflect the growth and decline of traits over time.

In brief, then, the states we should measure are those which have appeared in dR and R analyses, eliminating what appear to be change factors. Thus according to Cattell attempts to measure states or moods using R factor analyses alone cannot be trusted because the factors could be trait factors. On this rationale Cattell and his colleagues have produced two measures of states.

1   The Eight-State Questionnaire (Curran and Cattell, 1974) which measures: state extraversion, state anxiety, depression, arousal, fatigue, guilt stress and regression.
2   The Central State-Trait Kit (Barton and Cattell, 1981) which measures the five largest second-order state factors: extraversion, anxiety, arousal, alertness, independence and conscientiousness.

Comments on these Tests

The rationale of these tests, which has been discussed in detail above, is impeccable. However, they have not been much used and the evidence for the validity of these scales is not large. Furthermore, as was demonstrated in Chapter 6, the factor analytic solution of Cattell in the field of personality, which is the basis for these factors, is not regarded as satisfactory with the result that these state factors must also be treated with caution.

Examination of the factors themselves in the light of what are admittedly weak theories of motivation is not encouraging. Obviously state anxiety makes good sense but many of the other factors are not convincing *per se*. Indeed Boyle and Katz (1991) in an analysis of the 8SQ found two factors accounted for the variance – extraversion/arousal and negative state factors.

It must be concluded that Cattell's work on states is far from definitive and further research is required. Finally, it should be pointed out that Spielberger et al. (1970) have developed a state–trait anxiety inventory which is similar to the corresponding Cattell scales and this is a convenient and widely used test.

Other Factor Analyses of Moods and States

There are other factor analytic studies of moods and states but since these use R factoring, I shall not examine them in any detail (for example, Clyde, 1963 and Howarth, 1980). Generally in the study of moods by R analysis, the items used in the scales are similar to those of personality trait tests except that the items are in the present tense. Thus 'I am often miserable' would be a trait item and 'I am miserable now' would be the corresponding state. This sounds impressive but Watson (1988) showed that there was little difference in the results regardless of what tense was used in the item. This is another reason for not relying on R technique in the measurement of moods.

However, despite these difficulties with R analysis Watson and Tellegen (1985) surveyed all studies of mood up to that date and carried out some of their own factor analyses. They found two orthogonal factors accounted for much of the variance in mood scales: positive affect on which all the pleasant moods and states loaded and negative affect on which the unpleasant scales loaded. This result is interesting for two reasons. First, the finding that negative and positive affects are not opposites to each other but are separate independent factors and second, the fact that this result is similar to the analysis of the 8SQ by Boyle and Katz (1991). Cooper and McConnville (1989) demonstrated that the positive affect factor was similar to state extraversion and the negative affect factor to state anxiety, a finding endorsed by Meyer and Shack (1989) who found this to be true of both state and trait anxiety and extraversion.

Conclusions Concerning the Factor Analysis of Moods and States

Despite the difficulties with R analysis and the sound arguments against its sole use in the study of moods, the best account of moods and states is that there are two independent factors, positive and negative affect, which correspond to state anxiety and extraversion. The first factor makes good sense. The second, however, seems less convincing. The field cries out for more P analyses.

The Factor Analysis of Drives

The factor analysis of drives is a field in which there is remarkably little work. Indeed Cattell and his colleagues are the only group to have made the attempt (Cattell and Child, 1975 and Cattell, 1985). In our discussion of the term 'drives' we noted the difficulty that there was no agreement as to what are the main drives in human behaviour and the problem of the circularity of the term. This is why most researchers have eschewed the field.

The nub of the problem lies in deciding what variables to factor. Cattell's solution (Cattell, 1985) was one essentially taken from McDougall, namely to argue that drives underly attitudes and thus a study of attitudes could form the basis for the analysis of drives. Drives have three aspects: a tendency to attend to certain stimuli; each drive has a characteristic emotion, for example sexual arousal; there is an impulse to a particular action. Attitudes can tap drives because (Cattell and Child, 1975) strength of attitudes reflects the strength of impulses to action in response to a stimulus. 'In these circumstances (stimulus) I (organism) want (need) so much (of a certain intensity) to do this (specific goal, response) with that (relevant object).' This definition of attitudes fits closely with their concept of drives and forms the basis of their factor analysis. It is the motivational sphere. It must be noted that this definition of attitudes involves interests and this gives a clue that studies of time and effort spent in pursuing interests and objectives could give a good indication of attitudes and drives.

The Variables used in the Study of Attitudes and Drives

Cattell and Child (1975) extracted from the research into motivations and interests 68 indices which they felt could indicate strength of drives and the drives themselves. These included, for example, physiological measures, such as eye dilation, levels of information and better memory for material relevant to the attitude. All these are examples of objective tests, discussed in Chapter 6.

Before describing the findings from the factor analysis of these objective indices of interests and attitudes a further point needs to be made about drives. As McDougall (1932), Murray (1938) and Freud (1933) all argue, and this is the theoretical basis of Cattell's work (it is not simply empirical), not only are drives reflected in interests, but various behaviours can be traced back to certain goals and the same behaviour can be related to several goals. This is a point well understood in the advertising industry. Cars are an outstanding example, as I have argued previously (Kline, 1993). Thus among the reasons for buying an expensive car are: to impress colleagues at work; to arouse envy in neighbours; to feel powerful; to exhibit wealth; to demonstrate taste; to attract women or men. Many of these reasons are unconscious, not simply explicit. To a sociobiologist car purchase of this kind is a demonstration, ultimately, of alpha apedom, a belief that is surprisingly uncomforting awaiting breakdown rescue in the rain as a Rolls sweeps by. If goals are examined they are found to be hierarchically ordered: each leads back to a goal more remote until at lasts it stops. These final, ultimate goals are usually biological drives – hunger, thirst, sexual release – and are labelled by Cattell as ergs. In addition there are basic cultural drives – the sentiments.

This is the theoretical and psychometric background to Cattell's work on drives and strength of interests – objective tests derived from dynamic motivational theory subjected to simple structure factor analysis.

Motivational Strength Factors

- Alpha. This is called conscious id in that it reflects the satisfaction of personal desires, often against all sense. This is most commonly seen in sexual liaisons which are bound to bring disaster.
- Beta. Realised integrated interest. This is the component tapped in standard attitude questionnaires.
- Gamma. Superego. This is the moral component of interest, seen in the *Guardian* readers who care so deeply for the poor, the dispossessed, the environment and the champagne they sip as they think these noble thoughts.
- Delta. This reflects the physiological responses to stimuli.
- Epsilon. This is a conflict factor which Cattell and Child (1975) argue is related to repression.
- There were two other unidentified factors: zeta and eta.
- Second-order factors. There were two identifiable second-order factors – an integrated component loading beta and gamma, the conscious aspects of interests; and an unintegrated component loading alpha, delta and epsilon. This reflects the unconscious aspects of drives and interests.

Comments on these Factors

There are several important points about this research which require discussion.

- Cattell uses psychoanalytic terms to describe these factors and, as has been argued (Kline, 1981), this factor analysis does broadly fit a psychoanalytic model. However, this fit is not precise, for example the alpha factor is conscious, not unconscious. However, it shows that strength of interest is not unidimensional and is, at least in part, below the level of awareness, which ought not to be surprising because often we don't know why we like things: we just do.
- These findings are of great significance for the measurement of attitudes. Standard attitude questionnaires use face-valid items which must at best tap only the beta and gamma components, the latter,

incidentally, reflecting social desirability, which was discussed in Chapter 6. This means that they are far too simple-minded to be useful and account for the deficiencies of market research and political polling. In the light of these findings, attitude questionnaires must be treated with great caution.

- These factors, despite their profound implications for the measurement and understanding of interests, drives and attitudes have been neglected almost entirely by workers uninfluenced by Cattell. This means that there is insufficient evidence to be at all confident that these factors are valid. These are pioneering studies which have not been followed up. However, there is one published test, the Motivational Analysis Test (Cattell et al., 1970) which does measure the second-order factors as well as the main ergs and sentiments and these must now be examined.

Drive Factors: Ergs and Sentiments

A good account of these factors is to be found in Sweney et al. (1986) (ergs) and Gorsuch (1986) (sentiments).

Ten ergs are considered to be replicated. These are set out below.

Food seeking	Escape to security
Mating	Self-assertion
Gregariousness	Narcissistic sex
Parental pity	Pugnacity
Exploration	Acquistiveness

There are six other far more tentative ergs, particularly the last two. These are:

Appeal	Constructiveness
Rest seeking	Self-abasement
Laughter	Disgust

Eight sentiments have been identified.

Career	Self-sentiment
Home–parental	Sport and games
Mechanical	Sweetheart–spouse
Religious	Superego

Comments on these Ergs and Sentiments

It is clear from Cattell and Child (1975), Cattell (1985), Gorsuch (1986) and Sweney et al. (1986) that the evidence for the validity of these ergs and sentiments, including those which have been confidently labelled, is far less than for the ability and personality factors in the Cattell system. Certainly they have not been broadly accepted into psychometrics.

On account of the tentative nature of these factors I shall not say much about them. However, it is to be noted that these analyses strongly suggest that the motivational theorists were wrong. Thus McDougall (1932) and Murray (1938) postulated a considerably greater number of drives than is found here although Gorsuch (1986) argues that there are probably more sentiments than are included in this list. Conversely psychoanalytic drive theory (Freud, 1933) postulates too few factors, concentrating as it does on sex and aggression or at a more abstract level, eros and thanatos.

There can be no doubt that the measurement of drives is essential for the proper psychometric analysis of behaviour and the factor analytic approach must be the way forward. For this reason I shall also briefly discuss the two tests which Cattell and his colleagues use in the attempt to measure these variables. For here, in the motivational sphere, more research is required.

- The Motivational Analysis Test (MAT) (Cattell et al., 1970). This is an objective test of the questionnaire type where it is virtually impossible for subjects to guess what the questions are measuring. For example, they have to estimate the percentages of people who are happy to give money to a charity and there are forced choice items where subjects have to choose the better use of some commodity. The best five established ergs (mating, assertiveness, fear, comfort-seeking and pugnacity) and the best five established sentiments (self-sentiment, superego, career, sweetheart–spouse and parental–home) are measured by the test. In addition the two second-order strength of drive factors, previously discussed, can be measured. Kline (1999) summarised the evidence for the validity of the MAT which is far from convincing. However, one study of this test with my colleague Cooper (Kline and Cooper, 1982) demonstrated that this test needs considerable revision before it could be used with any confidence. A simple structure rotated factor analysis with the 16PF personality test (see Chapter 6) failed to yield any sensible factors and an item analysis of the ten scales showed that they were not homogeneous, at least in the British samples.
- The Vocational Interest Measure (VIM) (Sweney and Cattell, 1980). This is the attempt by Cattell to use his factor analytic work on motivation in the applied field. The VIM measures a selection of ergs

and sentiments which are as close as possible to the notion of interests which are seen as relevant by test users in industrial psychology. This test, therefore, bridges the gap between drives as ergs and sentiments and drives as interests which will be discussed in the next section. Two ergs and eight sentiments are measured by the VIM which, as with the MAT, is an objective test.

Variables in the VIM

Ergs: Protectiveness; rest seeking.
Sentiments: Career; clerical-work interests; aesthetic–dramatic interests; sports interests; mechanical interests; scientific interests; business interests; nature–outdoor interests.

Discussion of the VIM

This is the only objective test designed for applied psychology. However, as Sweney et al. (1986) make clear, there is insufficient evidence for its validity to enable it to be used with any confidence. This is a test which, because it is an objective test and rooted in Cattell's motivational theories (Cattell, 1985), deserves investigation and, if required and possible, modification and revision to improve its reliability and validity.

Conclusion Concerning the Study of Drives

As indicated, Cattell's approach is unique. It is interesting because of its reliance on the factor analysis of objective tests and the fact that the variables have been woven into a quantitative theory of motivation – the dynamic calculus (1985). However, far more work is required to ascertain the validity of these tests and any theorising is thus premature, although it demonstrates well the psychometric approach to motivation.

Psychometric Measurement of Interests

Despite the fact that Cattell (Cattell and Child, 1975, Cattell and Kline, 1977) had shown that direct questions about interests were unlikely to be useful because they tapped only the realised component of interests, the conscious aspects, the majority of interest tests are of this kind. In the main they are of little theoretical significance although Holland (1985b) has attempted to develop from his tests a theory of vocational choice.

Since, as has been made clear in Kline (1999) and Schmidt and Hunter (1998), these tests are not powerful for selection, I shall in this Primer briefly list and describe some of the most commonly used interest tests.

The Strong Vocational Interest Blank (SVIB) (Strong et al., 1971) and its modern form the Strong–Campbell Interest Inventory (Strong and Campbell, 1974)

The original test (Strong, 1927) was an outstanding example of a criterion-keyed test (see Chapter 4). Occupational interests are measured by comparing the responses to the items with the scores of 57 female and 67 male occupational groups. In the Inventory there are in addition six general occupational scales: realistic, investigative, artistic, social, enterprising and conventional. In addition, based upon correlated items, there 23 basic interest scales such as agriculture, nature, social services and so on. However, these scales are difficult to analyse since they share items, of which there are 399 in the SVIB and 327 in the Inventory. Despite its wide use the evidence for the validity of these tests is not outstanding. Katz (1972) showed that the scales had no higher validity than asking subjects what they were interested in. As Sweney et al. (1986) argue this test is probably useful as a basis for the discussion of occupational interests but not as a psychometric measure.

The Kuder Tests

These tests deserve mention because they have been extensively used, especially in America. The Kuder General Interest Survey (Kuder, 1970a) measures ten areas of interest – outdoor, mechanical, computational, scientific, persuasive, artistic literary, musical, social service and clerical – with 168 items. The Kuder Occupational Interest Survey (Kuder, 1970b) has 77 male occupational scales and 57 female occupational scales, all from 100 items. In both tests each item is a triad of activities and subjects have to indicate the most and least liked. Scoring a test in this way is, of course, ipsative scoring and the problems with this have been fully discussed in Chapter 4: the scores are negatively correlated and factor analysis is impossible; and norms are not meaningful. This means that the KGIS is only suitable for discussion with subjects. This item format is not so disadvantageous in the Occupational Survey since items were included in a scale if a particular group made such a choice. However, this means that many scales share items and this form of the Kuder is highly similar to the Strong Inventory discussed above and has all the same problems of validity.

The Vocational Preference Inventory (VPI) (Holland, 1985a)

This test was first introduced in 1953 and it stems from a huge programme of research into vocational preference (Holland 1985b). The test consists of 160 occupational titles to which subjects indicate like or dislike. From these choices 11 scales similar to those in the other interest tests which have been described – the six scales used in the Strong–Campbell Interest

Inventory plus self-control, masculinity, status and two psychometric check scores – infrequency and acquiescence. There are more than 400 investigations reported and discussed in Holland (1985b) concerning the validity of these scales. It can be said that there are moderate correlations with job choice and the Holland scores and that the scales are satisfactorily reliable. Studies with other tests suggest that there is some overlap with personality and Costa et al. (1984) have claimed that the big five factors (see Chapter 6) account for much of the variance in this test. Holland has developed a vocational theory which states that subjects tend to choose occupations which suit their personality, the theoretical but unremarkable basis of this test.

Conclusions

These tests are simple attempts to identify interests using face-valid items. The VPI is probably the best of these tests because it has some sensible theoretical support, does not use ipsative scoring and is not based upon criterion keying with all its disadvantages (see Chapter 4).

Attitude Measurement

In this final section I shall discuss the measurement of attitudes. The number of published scales is small on account of the fact that attitude measurement is not commercially attractive and most attitude scales are produced in the course of research by social psychologists. These tests may be found in the relevant articles but a great number of them have been collected together with critical comments by Robinson et al. (1991) which is an excellent source of such tests.

This discussion will be brief because the measurement of attitudes, as it is currently conceived, is weakened by the fact that it assumes that attitudes are entirely conscious and can be measured with face-valid items, the point made by Cattell (1985) and discussed above in our study of motivation. In fact there are three different methods of measuring attitudes and these will be scrutinised in turn.

Thurstone Attitude Scales

In Thurstone scales statements relevant to the attitude to be measured are collected, from books or newspapers, for example. These statements are rated by judges on an 11-point scale from 'strongly favourable' to 'strongly unfavourable'. Statements on which judges agree and which cover the whole range of attitude from 1 to 11 then form the test. The test score is either the mean rating of the items with which the subject agrees or the highest rating of any item which a subject endorses.

There are practical problems with these scales, notably that a large number of judges is required (100) for reliable ratings and these judges must represent the population for whom the test is intended or the ratings will again be inaccurate. There is a theoretical objection pointed out by Nunnally (1978), namely that each item should receive the keyed response only at a particular point on the attitude dimension. However, this is not so since if an item is endorsed at a point all those beyond this point will also endorse it. For these reasons Thurstone scales are not to be recommended.

Guttman Scales

In Guttman scaling items are so ordered in terms of the attitude that if a subject endorses item 5, for example, she will also endorse items 1, 2 and 3 and 4. If a subject gets item 9 wrong then all subsequent items will be wrong. Thus each item is perfectly correlated with the total score.

Such a scale is intuitively appealing and it does mean that whatever a subject scores, the tester knows what items were correct and what were not. This is not so on a conventional test. However, there are problems with Guttman scaling. For example, as Levy (1973) points out, it is unlikely that in the real world any item would correlate perfectly with the total score. The underlying model is not realistic. Perhaps more importantly Guttman scaling depends on the difficulty level of the items (see Chapter 4). This means that there is no guarantee of unidimensionality which was shown to be essential for measurement. It is possible to form a Guttmann scale from a disparate collection of items. Finally, as Levy (1973) points out, the measurement provided by Guttman scales is only ordinal and this restricts statistical analyses and scientific inferences, as was discussed in Chapter 2. For these reasons Guttman scales are hard to recommend.

Likert Scales

Likert (1932) developed the form of attitude scale which bears his name. This consists of attitude statements followed by a five- or seven-point rating scale indicating the degree of agreement or disagreement with the scale. Such tests can be developed using the techniques of item analysis or factor analysis which were discussed in Chapter 4. Likert scales are used by most social psychologists who need to measure attitudes.

Conclusions Concerning Attitude Scales

From this discussion it is clear that Thurstone and Guttman scales have too many problems to make them useful methods of measuring attitudes and Likert scales are widely used. However, as has been discussed these measure only the conscious, integrated component of attitudes, and for this reason are likely to be somewhat superficial.

Finale

In this chapter we have scrutinised the meaning and measurement of motivation and attitudes. However conceptualised, as drives, states, moods or interests, the measurement of motivation has not yielded an agreed set of findings. Factor analysis of the motivational sphere has hardly begun and all these dynamic factors require more than R factor analysis for clear identification. Positive and negative mood factors are perhaps the clearest finding in this field. Interest tests are too simple even if useful in practice. Similarly attitude scaling, although widely used in social psychology, still deals only with the conscious aspects of attitude and this is a weakness, as has been discussed.

8
Psychometric Testing in Applied Psychology

There are three main fields of applied psychology in which psychometrics plays a part – educational, clinical and occupational/organisational psychology. There are many books about each of these applications and huge amounts of research so that to deal adequately with such a corpus of work in this Primer plainly would be impossible.

Nevertheless it is possible to discuss briefly the contributions of psychometrics to these areas of psychology by elucidating the principles and approaches in their application and by illustrating these with examples of such work. Furthermore such examples need not be restricted to what has been achieved but what might be achieved given the principles which have been elucidated.

Educational Psychology

Educational psychology can be defined as the use of psychology to improve education, both its organisation and, of greater psychological and intellectual interest, its dealings with individual children who are having problems at school. My discussion will be concerned mainly with the second aspect of educational psychology, although clearly any findings must have repercussions on the first.

It should be made clear at the outset that I am not going to discuss current educational psychology as it is practised either here or in any other country. Such practice is inevitably limited by the finances made available to the service, the training and calibre of the practitioners and what happens to be politically acceptable. I intend to scrutinise how psychometrics could be used to solve educational problems. Of course such an approach will be relevant to current practice, as will be seen.

The Psychometric Model and Educational Psychology

The psychometric model was explicated in Chapter 6. This states that any behaviour is a function of ability, personality, motivation and situation, although in psychometrics the latter is usually omitted. In educational psychology this situational variable is, of course, constant, being the educational institution, and this can be investigated. Such a model is so inclusive as to be bound to be true and is thus of little value unless it can be made operational. As I hope is now clear from the preceding chapters of this Primer, factor analysis has made it possible to instantiate the model, since through factor analysis the major variables in each of these fields – ability, personality and motivation, have been identified. Indeed the huge programme of research by Cattell was specifically aimed to elucidate and make operational the psychometric model which could then be applied to any aspect of human behaviour. That there is not complete agreement that Cattell did correctly identify the main factors is not the point. What is important is the principle of applying this psychometric model of behaviour using factored variables.

The Relevance of the Psychometric Model to Educational Psychology

In educational psychology the use of the psychometric model has been in the prediction and understanding of educational success, the selection of students and the diagnosis and identification of educational problems. Although these are not unrelated I shall discuss each separately. However, before I do this I want to comment briefly upon some of the major psychometricians.

Burt (despite the misdemeanours in his studies of twins which render that work valueless) made a huge contribution both to the development of psychometrics with many tests and theoretical advances in methods (for example, Burt, 1940) and to educational psychology itself. He was the inventor of the profession and set up the first educational psychological service in London. Burt was not simply a statistical and psychometric expert. His practical experience informs all his work. This is true of many of the leading British psychometrists. Thus Cattell set up the Leicester Child Guidance Service and Vernon also had practical experience with children. I believe that this has had the effect of making their theoretical work highly relevant to educational psychology and Vernon was, indeed, for many years in the Institute of Education in London.

Prediction of Academic Success

The application of the model to predicting academic success is quite straightforward. All that is required is a multiple correlation (see Glossary) between examination scores and ability, personality and motivational factors.

Results

As I indicated earlier in this chapter there is a huge amount of research in this field which could not be discussed in detail in the Primer, or indeed in any one book. However, summaries of the research findings can be found in Jensen (1980), Kline (1993) and Mackintosh (1998) in respect of intelligence and Kline (1979) with regard to motivational and personality factors. Cattell and Johnson (1986) also contains much relevant information as do the handbooks to Cattell's personality tests. A more detailed account of this work can be found in Kline (1999).

A possible method of summarising all this research would be to conduct a meta-analysis. However, much of the published research in this field is of a low standard, the results of empiricism run mad where correlations between academic success and a huge range of tests were computed, often with large samples. As a result correlations of a very small size, for example .18, are significant and in addition with so many variables some correlations are significant by chance. Thus one researcher (who is best left nameless) found that Cattell's H, adventurousness, correlated .21 with German O-level but not with French. Interpretation of such tiny correlations of this kind are highly dubious. In addition there are problems with the reliability of the tests and the criteria. These are low, which renders the correlations lower than they might be. On the other hand, corrections for attenuation due to unreliability may be unrealistic. All these difficulties make meta-analyses of little value. Instead I have attempted to summarise those results which do appear to meet the technical criteria of good research and which have been replicated, often many times. The results are set out below.

- Intelligence is the best single predictor of academic success. As Jensen (1980) has shown, intelligence is the best single predictor of academic success at all levels. Vernon (1961) also showed this to be the case and such findings were the basis of using the intelligence tests in selection for grammar schools in Great Britain before the advent of comprehensive education. It was also demonstrated by Vernon that the effects of social economic class on intelligence were far smaller than was the case with attainment tests or any other kind of selection procedure. Thus IQ tests were a fair method of selection for disadvantaged children. Obtained correlations with academic success, particularly at the university level, are often small but significant. However, this results from attenuation due to homogeneity of variance. Thus when only a small proportion of an age group went to university the range of intelligence was narrow and this reduces correlations. In modern universities this spread of intelligence is greater although as yet it does not embrace those low in intelligence (although the effusions of academics in the social sciences might well lead one to the opposite conclusion). One might therefore expect correlations with academic success to rise although this is offset by the fact that many degree subjects require little g to complete them. The work by Cattell and Butcher (1968) is a clear illustration of the predictive power of intelligence both at the secondary and higher education levels.

- Verbal and numerical factors are also important in relevant academic subjects. These two factors are important in the prediction of Arts and Science subjects respectively. This is hardly surprising in the light of experience but this is sometimes not supported by research. However, the notion of highly verbal and highly scientific individuals, exemplified by, say, Shakespeare and Newton, makes good sense

- Personality variables have small but significant correlations with academic success. Cattell and Butcher (1968) again have typical results. At secondary school and university, extraversion and anxiety, the two main personality factors, as was discussed in Chapter 6, correlate about .25 with academic performance. This is true even in countries other than Europe, as, for example, I found in Ghana (Kline, 1966). What this means is that a moderate degree of anxiety is helpful for doing well at school and university, presumably because without anxiety, subjects tend not to worry about poor work and the displeasure of their teachers. On the other hand, too much anxiety is bad for examination performance, as Vernon (1963) confirms. As regards extraversion the results differ among the age groups. At secondary school and university the stable introvert does best but at the primary school the advantage lies with the stable extravert. This probably reflects the different teaching methods for primary and secondary children, the former encouraging movement and discussion, the latter favouring the bookish temperament. It should be noted that G, superego, in the Cattell system also correlates positively with academic success (Cattell, 1973). However, this is of less interest since it reflects only the fact that conscientious children tend to do better. Thus, to conclude, it can be seen that personality factors correlate moderately with academic performance but the variance for which they account is different from that of ability tests.

- Small correlations can be observed between academic performance and motivational factors. The motivational factors isolated by Cattell (Cattell and Child, 1975, Cattell, 1985) also have small correlations with academic success, as found by Cattell and Butcher (1968). The relevant motivational factors were self-assertiveness, superego and narcissistic sex. Indeed Cattell (1985) claims that these variables have large beta weights in the specification equation for academic success. However, given the problems with these motivational factors and the fact that the Cattell and Butcher study, excellent as it is, has not been replicated, some caution about beta weights need to be shown. What seems clear, however, is that these motivational factors account for different variance from that of either personality or ability in the prediction of academic achievement.

- Conclusions concerning the prediction of academic performance. There is no doubt that ability, personality and motivational factors can together account for a substantial proportion of the variance in academic success. The multiple correlation is around .65. Given other factors that must affect school performance, for example teachers, peer groups, encouragement at home, this result is impressive. As Cattell (1973, 1985) argues, specification equations showing the optimum weightings for the factors could be obtained with a variety of educational performance measures and these weights would be likely to differ for different courses of study. Such a set of specification equations would not only improve the prediction of educational achievement but would add substantially to our understanding of academic performance because, it must be remembered, factored variables are meaningful, since by definition they account for the most variance in their fields. Thus with the psychometric model and substantial research specification equations for academic success could be developed which would begin to make educational psychology scientific and rational. They would also form the basis for work in the other endeavours of educational psychology, which will now be discussed.

Selection of Students

The findings which have been discussed in the previous section and which demonstrate beyond doubt that academic performance can be predicted from psychometric tests also form the basis for the use of psychometric tests in educational selection. From these results it is clear that an intelligence test is the single most useful test in selection but selection could be improved if personality and motivational measures were also used. These claims, in the light of the correlations discussed previously, are unequivocal and in the rest of this section I shall discuss some of the objections which have been raised to these apparently rational arguments.

- All selection for education, especially at school, is invidious. Pedley (1955) makes this point clearly in his arguments on behalf of comprehensive school education. He claims that psychologists have for too long sacrificed at the mystic altar of IQ and that, in fact, the reality of failure at 11, as it is perceived by the child, and its consequent damage, far outweigh all other aspects of selection. I shall say little about this argument other than to note that is it essentially a moral one about which a scientific psychology can have nothing to say. Psychometrics enables one to predict academic performance. What is done with such a potential is not a question of psychology but morality.

- Selection by psychometric tests is unfair, reflecting social class and other discriminatory factors rather than ability. This is a further argument which is sometimes implicit in the arguments against the use of intelligence tests in selection. However, this is simply incorrect and is contraverted by the evidence which I shall now discuss, point by point. Readers may be surprised by the fact that this evidence is old but this is because these issues were settled beyond reasonable doubt early in the development of psychological testing. Excellent summaries of this evidence can be found in Vernon (1961) and Jensen (1980).

- Intelligence test scores and social class. It is sometimes argued that intelligence tests favour the children of well-educated parents. However, as Vernon (1961) makes clear, any such effects are small compared with any other measure of educational attainment or intellectual potential. Thus one of the originators of factor analysis and intelligence testing in Great Britain, Godfrey Thomson, developed intelligence tests to select miners' children from Durham mining communities precisely because before this no children qualified for grammar school education. The majority of children selected this way achieved well, as is to be expected in the light of the evidence in the previous section. Yet on attainment tests such children performed poorly. This directly refutes this claim.

- Intelligence tests are another form of attainment test so that performance on such tests simply reflects educational opportunities. This again is easily refuted. As Vernon (1960) demonstrates there is relatively little improvement as a result of coaching and practice in intelligence tests. Furthermore what improvement there is comes after a maximum of six hours' coaching. This indicates that the ability to reason is not simply learned as bits of history or sociology, which no doubt would respond to such coaching. It implies that reasoning ability is a function of the brain, which, given a normal environment, develops regardless, much as other biological functions. This is supported by the fact that such improvements do not generalise across different intelligence tests.

- There is an overlap between the content of intelligence tests and tests of educational attainment. In one sense this must be true or there would be no correlation. This apparent overlap reflects the application of an individuals general reasoning ability within the educational learning domain. Evidence for this comes from the fact that the intelligence test is the best predictor of how easily and well an individual will learn a totally new subject, for example Japanese, as Jensen (1980) fully explicates.

- Performance on intelligence tests and measures of educational attainment are correlated because of motivational factors. This argument attempts to explain the results on the grounds that some individuals are motivated to try hard at all tests and others, disadvantaged people, are not. This is nonsense in the light of the evidence. If this were the case intelligence test scores would correlate equally with all attainments, which is not the case. Furthermore all attempts to measure motivation and personality indicate clearly that such variables are not correlated with intelligence (see Cattell, 1957). Finally, the work of Cattell and Butcher (1968) showed that motivational variables and intelligence account for different parts of the variance of educational attainment.

Conclusions Concerning the Use of Intelligence Tests in Educational Selection

There is no doubt that intelligence test scores correlate positively with educational success. Thus if selection is desired intelligence test scores are the best indicator, which can be improved by using further psychometric tests. This correlation reflects the fact that intelligence tests measure reasoning ability which is important in most worthwhile educational attainments. It is clear that the observed correlation does not reflect social class differences between individuals, differences in educational attainment or motivation or previous practice at intelligence tests. As Vernon (1960) concluded, intelligence tests provide the fairest and most valid means of selection for education which has ever been devised.

There is one argument for the use of intelligence tests in selection for education which is rarely discussed by those opposed to them. As Jensen (1980) argues, intelligence is related to the speed and ease of learning. This means that children are most easily taught in groups which are homogeneous for intelligence. There can be fast and slow streams and this ought to ensure that children all proceed at a pace right for them. It eliminates the boredom for bright children of the slow lesson and the horror for the less bright of total incomprehension. But this is heresy!

The Diagnosis and Identification of Educational Problems

In the early days of educational psychology the educational psychologist was recognisable from the little brown case which he always carried. This was the WISC test. Intelligence testing was seen as the key to educational diagnosis and the rationale for this view is easily to be found in the correlations which were discussed at the beginning of this chapter and also in the psychometric model.

The argument runs thus. The performance of a child at school is to a large part determined by intelligence. Obviously other factors, such as parental attitudes, peer groups, teachers and the interests and personality of the child have some influence, but, as the evidence shows, intelligence is the single best predictor of academic success. Furthermore, as Jensen (1980) and Vernon (1961) make clear, intelligence has a causal role: it sets a limit as to what may be achieved. With such a view of intelligence, the psychometric view, the intelligence test is crucial for diagnosis, as a few simple examples will illustrate.

Suppose a child is sent to the educational psychologist because she is performing poorly at school. Now it is obvious that until the intelligence of the child is known her performance cannot be properly judged. Suppose the child is having great difficulty, in an old-fashioned school, with geometric problems. Unlike her 13-year old peers she is overwhelmed by Pythagoras and trigonometry. If she turns out to have an IQ of 90 we can feel confident that the subject matter is probably the cause. It is too hard for her, at least as it is taught in that school. She can be given an easier syllabus or more time and teaching to learn what is required. However, if it turns out that her IQ is 125 then we can be confident that this is not the reason for failure. She ought to have no problems. Hence we can start to investigate other reasons for failures – problems at home, difficulties with the teacher and so on.

In fact, the proper use of intelligence tests, contrary to the dogma of the left, for example Pedley (1955), is not cruel and heartless. It is so to try to force children to learn things beyond their capabilities, as in our previous example. So too is the converse as Burt (1940) made clear when he portrayed the boredom of very bright children taught as is suitable for children of average ability.

I think that this is sufficient to indicate that to attempt to understand learning difficulties without recourse to IQ tests is difficult and of dubious rationale. Of course it is not suggested that the application of one intelligence test is the end of the matter. It is not. However, it forms a solid basis for further investigations. What these might be, however, cannot be dealt with in this Psychometrics Primer. Suffice it to say that to qualify as an educational psychologist demands an intensive course of post-graduate study. In this Primer I am concerned simply to demonstrate how the psychometric model can (and should) inform the practice of educational psychology. It is also pertinent to point out that other psychometric tests can be useful.

For example, highly introverted children are likely to need different teaching styles from extraverts and this could be a cause of difficulty. In addition very useful diagnostic tests for Primary English and Mathematics have been developed by Schonell and Schonell (1950) which can pinpoint precise sources of confusion.

Conclusions Concerning the Diagnosis of Educational Problems

In this brief section I have indicated how the psychometric model has important implications in diagnosing the causes of educational difficulties and that intelligence testing both theoretically and on empirical grounds appears to be essential. Other tests are also important, as in the work of Cattell and Butcher (1968), and for a more detailed treatment of the application of tests for these purposes readers are referred to Cattell and Johnson (1986).

Finale: Psychometric Tests and Education

Although in this Primer I have not been able to do more than outline some main findings and principles, it is clear that psychometrics has important implications for education. It is useful in the prediction and understanding of educational success and effective in selection. There can be no doubt that intelligence is a determinant of educational success. Furthermore the application of tests is useful for the problems presented in educational psychology.

Psychometrics and Occupational Psychology

This is another huge field of psychology in which, as was the case with education, I shall eschew details but attempt to discuss the principles and rationale of psychometrics. Occupational psychology, at least in the UK, is a rapidly growing field but it is not growing in the same way in the USA simply because it is already so well established there. However, although many tests are given in the course of occupational psychology, sufficient to make test constructors millionnaires, there seem to be many departures from the implications of the psychometric model and psychometric rigour. Here I shall discuss how psychometrics can make a genuine and valuable contribution to occupational psychology.

Psychometric Testing and Occupational Selection

The psychometric model implies that behaviour is a function of ability, personality and motivational variables, taking into account the context of behaviour involved. Thus if we know the demands of a job in terms of personality and ability and we can test individuals for these variables, then job selection becomes entirely rational and this is the basis for using psycho-metric tests in occupational selection.

How this simple principle is put into practice is set out below and there are several different approaches. More detailed discussions of these methods can be found in Cook (1998), Furnham (1995) and Smith and Robertson (1989).

An Idealised Approach

More than 20 years ago I proposed (Kline, 1979) on the basis of the psy-chometric model that an encyclopedia of job specifications be set up. These specifications would be in terms of the major factored variables in the fields of personality, ability and motivation, specifically their regression weights in the prediction of occupational success. The major factors, as has been argued, are the most important and psychologically significant variables in their sphere. Thus from such an encyclopedia, as it was built up, a theory of occupational success could be developed. This would mean that the demands of new jobs could be understood and job analyses would not have to be done as a basis for selection. Furthermore the design of the working environment could be theoretically based and result in improved efficiency and occupational satisfaction. Such an encyclopedia, it was argued, could be developed by collecting and collating the data from all work in the personnel field. However, no such encyclopedia exists and we have to make do with the findings published in journals or in the manuals to psycho-logical tests. In these there are various different approaches which will be discussed below.

Predicting Occupational Success

As was argued above this was to be the basis of the encyclopedia of job spec-ifications. In this method a battery of psychological tests is applied together with criterion measures of occupational success. The beta weights of the regression equation indicate the salient variables in success and it is these which are used in the selection procedure. The problem with this approach is that it is not always easy to establish adequate criteria for occupational success, especially in jobs where outcomes are complex, as in teaching, for example.

Discriminating Criterion Groups

This method involves testing large numbers of different occupational groups and producing profiles of scores for each group. Thus Cattell et al. (1970) in the handbook to the 16PF have a large number of such profiles and the selection procedure involves obtaining individuals with the best matched score profile to the appropriate group.

Comments on these Methods

I have already commented upon the problems of obtaining adequate criteria for success but other difficulties need mention. In both methods good sampling is essential. Thus electrical engineers, all from one large organisation, may not be representative of electrical engineers in general and this is important given that organisations tend to have their own individual cultures. In the case of the profile matching method there are two obvious difficulties. Not all members of any occupational group are well suited to the occupation or particularly successful at it. Furthermore jobs change with time and these methods inevitably involve matching individuals to old jobs. The introduction of computers, for example in libraries, certainly altered the job specifications of librarians, as, sadly, all library users must know.

Job Specifications and Job Analysis

The third common approach to the use of tests in job selection is to specify what a job demands in terms of traits and select individuals who best match these demands. Job and task analysis is not an easy matter and is outside the scope of this Primer. However, one test, the Position Analysis Questionnaire, the PAQ (McCormick et al., 1972), can be given to occupants of jobs and seems to have some validity in that its use improves selection. However, it has been argued (see Cook, 1998) that very simple job analyses, for example that a job is clerical, are just as effective. However, *a priori*, if job analyses are accurate and tests are good (very important conditions) this method should be effective.

The Effectiveness of Psychometric Tests in Job Selection

As has been argued there is one psychometric measure which stands out beyond all others in the prediction of occupational success – the intelligence test. Ghiselli (1966) found this correlation, with any job, to be around .3, on average, and a recent survey of 85 years of research by Schmidt and Hunter (1998) indicates that the correlation is even higher – .51. As is to be expected the correlation increases with the complexity of the job. However, excellent as this is, it is must be realised that for many positions, for example chemical engineering, the subjects, by virtue of possessing difficult professional qualifications, will all be highly intelligent and this correlation may not be that useful in practice. However, it is valuable, if unsurprising, in understanding what determines occupational success.

Personality tests and interest tests are not of great effectiveness in the prediction of occupational success despite their wide usage. The highest correlations are only in the order of .3 as many surveys have indicated, for example Barrick and Mount (1991), Salgado (1997). Of the personality variables the highest correlation is with conscientiousness – around .3. This is not surprising. In fact, it exemplifies a methodological error common in the social sciences, that of putting *a priori* propositions to the empirical test. It makes no sense to argue that a conscientious person would do any job less well than an unconscientious one, all other things being equal. It must be true. All correlations with other personality factors are smaller than this and are significant only in the statistical sense. Remember that even a correlation of .3 indicates less than 10% of variance in common. This small correlation size was regarded by Blinkhorn (for example, 1998) as evidence that they had arisen essentially by chance, given the large numbers of variables involved and the large number of investigations. This is certainly a viable case although Cattell always argued (for example, 1957) that although the correlations with personality were small in a multiple correlation with occupational success personality variables were useful because they accounted for variance different from that of intelligence tests.

There is one further point that should be borne in mind. These coefficients are averages. In some specific occupations job analysis may reveal that a personality variable is crucial and this may then be a valuable test for selection.

Conclusions Concerning the Efficiency of Psychometric Tests in Selection

In general only the intelligence test is effective. However, as has been argued, a multiple correlation with personality variables may increase the efficiency of selection and in specific cases the correct selection of ability and personality variables can result in higher coefficients than those discussed. If psychometric tests were used in the optimal way, that is weighted to maximise efficiency based on multiple regressions, these validity coefficients would appear more impressive and in any case they are reduced inevitably through homogeneity of variance, as has been discussed. Thus, in summary, it would be wrong, in personnel selection, to abandon the use of personality measures on account of these results. However, it seems equally misguided to utilise these tests before the correct weights have been established.

There is one final point. As was shown in our opening chapter, current psychometric tests are unlike the measures in the other sciences, having no units of measurement and not being ratio scales. If a more powerful New Psychometrics could be developed as I have advocated (Kline, 1998) great improvements might be realised and this possibility is briefly discussed in the next chapter.

Computerised Testing in Occupational Psychology

Before leaving the field of occupational psychology, I want to discuss, briefly, computerised psychometric testing, which is becoming increasingly important.

There are two kinds of computerised tests – conventional psychometric tests which are presented on a computer and tests specifically designed for computer presentation. I shall discuss each of these separately.

Conventional Psychometric Tests Presented on a Computer

Any tests can be presented on a computer, for example a personality questionnaire. The items will appear on the screen and subjects will be required to press designated keys to respond or a special response keyboard will be provided.

If a conventional test is presented on a computer it cannot be assumed that the reliability and validity or the norms remain the same. All these attributes need to be investigated. The correlation between the conventional and computerised should always be presented.

A problem with all computerised tests lies in the fact that the number of individuals who can be tested at once is limited by the number of available computers. There is a further practical problem that freedom from breakdown cannot, in my experience, be guaranteed, as many workers with computers of all kinds know to their costs. Finally there is a small number of subjects who are still computer-phobic and for these this form of presentation is obviously unsatisfactory. However, all these issues are relatively minor. They have been pointed out because they must not be ignored.

There are real advantages to computer presentation which apply also to tests designed from the outset to run on computers and I shall discuss these after I have scrutinised this second form of computerised testing.

Tests Specifically Designed for Computers

It is possible to write test items which could only be presented on computer. If they turn out to be valid this makes this kind of test indispensable. For example, many computer games require subjects to react quickly, to control moving points on the screen or hit targets. Similar tasks are used in computerised tests. In tests of spatial ability spatial transformations of figures are presented for recognition. For tests of perceptual speed words are degraded (in terms of pixels) and upgraded until subjects can read them. AGARD tests are typical computerised tests. Reaction times are measured in various tasks as is the skill to hit a target.

With tests of this kind, as with all tests, it is necessary to demonstrate that they are reliable and valid, and norms must be established. There is no magic about computerised tests. No test, of any kind, is anything more than a collection of items. The presentation, whether by pencil and paper or computer, is analogous to the binding of a book although certain items can only be presented by computer.

The Advantages of Computerised Testing

The great advantage of all forms of computerised testing lies in the rapidity with which the tests can be scored and feedback given to subjects, both highly valuable in the practice of occupational psychology.

Scoring and Interpretation

It is not just that the test can be automatically scored as the subject completes it but interpretations of the score can also be printed out. These are based on the norms to the test which are stored on disk. There is no magical computing here; the interpretative meanings to each score will also have been fed into the computer, ready for printing. Such interpretations depend entirely on the skill of the individual who wrote them. In good occupational psychology practice such printouts should always be discussed with subjects.

Research

Computerised testing is ideal for research. Thus item analyses can be automatic after a sufficient number of subjects have been built up and if results are systematically stored in a database, after several years' testing useful information can be obtained. Thus the efficiency of test items and scales can be easily investigated and the relation of the test scores to other criteria can be found. All this is possible with normal conventional testing but all the data has to be fed into the computer and this is often simply not done for obvious reasons of time and cost.

Conclusions Concerning Computerised Testing

As is clear computerised testing has three advantages. It allows the use of items which would otherwise be impossible, it provides immediate scoring and feedback and it enables research to be more easily undertaken. It might be added that it conveys to applicants, provided that it works, a feeling of modern high-tech efficiency. On the other hand, there is no magic in computerised testing. If the items are invalid the test will be useless and if the interpretation is poor it will be worthless no matter the beauty of the printout or the speed of its completion.

Psychometric Tests in Clinical Psychology

Clinical psychology is a topic of such complexity and disagreement among psychologists and also among psychiatrists that in this Primer a proper treatment of the use of psychometric tests is quite impossible. In this field we see all the disparate views which have rendered psychology so diverse. The claims of psychoanalysis, learning theories, pharmacological and genetic accounts (ignoring the horrors of social constructivists) are difficult to reconcile and each implies a different valuation of psychometric testing.

Thus in the concluding section of this chapter I shall do no more than sketch in how psychometric tests might be used, in the light of the psychometric model which has been fully elaborated above. Here the main exponent of the field is Cattell. In addition I shall briefly mention a few other uses of psychometric tests in clinical psychology.

Psychometric Tests in Clinical Diagnosis

Even if mental illness is not regarded as identical with physical illness, it makes sense to attempt to classify its many variations. Thus if the causes of depression and schizophenia are to be understood it is important that diagnosis of these syndromes be accurate and the same is true for other varieties of mental illness. Psychometric testing can offer two approaches to diagnosis which will be briefly described.

The Use of the Main Personality Factors

Cattell (for example, 1973 and Cattell and Kline, 1977) has argued that investigation of psychiatric groups with the best-known personality factors is of considerable psychological interest. Over the years Cattell and colleagues have carried out extensive factor analyses of the personality of clinical groups and this has resulted in the isolation of a number of abnormal factors, in addition to those of the 16PF test and they can all be measured in the Clinical Analysis Questionnaire, the CAQ (Krug, 1980).

The approach to diagnosis using this test is similar to the methods used for selection in occupational psychology. Thus a specification equation is drawn up with the beta weights for the various diagnostic groups. The scores of individuals are thus weighted and the highest resulting score indicates the diagnosis. Bolton (1986) contains examples of such specification equations. Alternatively profiles on the factors of the various groups can be obtained and profile matching between individuals' scores and these profiles also yields a diagnosis.

The great advantage of this general approach, compared with mere discrimination by any test or set of observations, is that these factors have psychological meaning and can, therefore, be used as the basis for clinical theorising. Indeed Krug (1986) has computerised this system producing an automatic diagnosis. At this point it should be made clear that, contrary to intuition and the claims of most clinicians, the abolition of subjective judgement in diagnosis is likely to yield more valid diagnoses not fewer, as Grove and Meehl (1996) have demonstrated.

The Use of other Tests

In clinical psychology and psychiatry workers and researchers have used psychometrics somewhat more pragmatically than the approach of Cattell, based upon the psychometric model. They have attempted to develop tests specifically to diagnose different disorders. The MMPI (Hathaway and McKinley, 1938), which has been discussed in this Primer as an example of criterion-keyed test construction, was designed for this purpose.

In an effort to overcome the unreliability of psychiatric diagnosis, in America a set of diagnostic criteria for various mental disorders has been developed over a number of years, largely based upon the presence or absence of certain symptoms. These are known as the DSM manuals and the latest version is DSM-IV (American Psychiatric Association, 1994). However, although such checklists can ensure reliability, their validity is dependent on whether, in fact, the symptoms truly form syndromes since there is no theoretical basis for these classifications. Despite this, efforts have been made to construct psychometric tests to aid diagnosis into the DSM categories.

Mathews and Deary (1998) contains a good summary of this work which is beyond the scope of this Primer to discuss in detail. It is sufficient to note that Millon (1983) developed the Millon Multiaxial Personality Inventory with 20 scales to fit these classifications and to measure other related variables such as therapeutic implications and personality patterns, all with 175 items. However, since the classification system is arbitrary, in the first place, I shall not discuss this test further.

Widiger and Costa (1994) found little empirical support for the classifications in DSM-IV and I shall not discuss this application of psychometric testing further. However, there have been attempts to investigate the factor structure of abnormal personality by workers in the clinical field. Livesley et al. (1992) developed the Dimensional Assessment of Personality–Pathology Basic Questionnaire which used factor analysis to investigate the classifications of the DSM system, writing items which appeared to tap the diagnostic criteria. Ultimately 16 factors were obtained. Schroeder et al. (1992) factored these scales along with the NEO (see Chapter 6) in a study of their validity. This study indicated that much of the variance in the D scales is similar to that of the NEO. For example, ten scales loaded the anxiety factor, and there were obvious extraversion, agreeableness and conscientiousness factors. Furthermore only seven of the scales were unifactorial and all this casts doubt on whether simple structure was obtained – a defect, as has been argued, which affects much of the research with the big five factors. For these reasons I shall not discuss this work further.

One further psychometric study of abnormal personality deserves mention – the work of Cloninger (1987) who developed the Tri-Dimensional Personality Questionnaire. Cloninger and colleagues attempted to measure abnormal factors which had some biological basis, which as has been argued in this Primer is an essential for a scientific psychometrics. Three factors were measured – novelty seeking, harm avoidance and reward dependence – all of which, they claim, are dependent on specific brain mechanisms. However, this claim is bound to be true. What is important is to be able to demonstrate precisely what these mechanisms are. In addition there is another important task: to establish that these factors are not simply other versions of neuroticism or anxiety, extraversion and some mix of the other factors so often found in personality questionnaires.

Conclusions Concerning the Use of Psychometric Tests in Clinical Diagnosis

Clearly this aspect of psychometrics is not well developed. No unequivocal findings have emerged from this work except that anxiety is an important factor in mental disorders and that psychosis differs from neurosis, as has been shown by Eysenck (1967a).

Other Uses of Psychometric Tests in Clinical Psychology

The chief use of psychometrics in clinical psychology is diagnostic – utilising, as has been seen, regression equations and other analogous statistical techniques to this end. However, for example, tests can be used in other ways. Cattell (e.g. 1973) argues that tests can be valuable in the evaluation of treatment. Thus, for example, if we know what personality factors are elevated in various mental disorders, successful treatment ought to result in changes on these factors and not simply in changes in symptoms. However, given the problems with the Cattell factors which have been discussed in this Primer, the rationale of the approach, rather than any detailed findings, is of interest.

Finally I want to mention projective tests. Despite all their defects of measurement which have been fully discussed in Chapter 6, clinicians do use these tests because of the insights which the responses to such tests appear to offer (see Exner (1986) in the manual to the Rorschach). It is possible that with objective scoring and rigorous statistical analyses such insights might be shown to have some validity. However, the warning of Grove and Meehl (1996) must not be forgotten: statistical prediction is better than subjective, at present the basis for using projective tests.

Conclusions Concerning the Use of Psychometric Tests in Applied Psychology

In all these fields, clinical, occupational and educational, the main application of psychometric tests lies in their ability to predict and to classify. Intelligence tests, measuring the g factors, are effective in the prediction of occupational and educational success. To a much lesser extent personality factors are useful in these respects. In clinical psychology there has been less success, partly because clinical psychologists tend not to like psychometric methods, although anxiety has been shown to be an important factor.

Apart from those with intelligence tests, these results have been disappointing given that psychometrics is about 100 years old. In Chapter 1 of this Primer I showed that psychometrics differs from the measures of the natural sciences and it is possible that if psychometric measurement were to become more scientific improvements could be made. In the final chapter I discuss some possible new approaches to psychological measurement – the New Psychometrics.

9
The New Psychometrics and Conclusions

In Chapter 2 of the Primer it was pointed out that psychometric measurement, although its avowed aim is to provide scientific measurement of psychological variables, was in fact quite different from the measurement of the natural sciences. In the sciences ratio scales are used with equal intervals and true zeros. Furthermore there is a clear unit of measurement. Indeed measurement essentially consists of estimating or computing the ratio of some unit of measurement to the object being measured. Such ratio scales with true zeros, equal intervals and units of measurement are known as fundamental or extensive measures. The measurement of length is a clear example of such a fundamental measure. In addition science makes use of derived measures which are some function of two fundamental measures as in the example of velocity. There is one further aspect of scientific measurement, as explicated by Michell (1990, 1997) and that is the necessity for demonstrating that the variable to be measured has a quantitative structure, which is an empirical issue, requiring evidence. It is clearly senseless to attempt to measure variables which have no such quantitative structure. It is, to conclude the arguments concerning measurement in the natural sciences, precisely the precision and meaningfulness of such measurement which lies at the heart of the advances in the natural sciences. If psychology is to advance as a science, such precise measurement is a necessity.

From our examination of the nature of psychometric tests, throughout every chapter of this Primer, it is clear that they differ considerably from measures in the natural sciences. Thus equal intervals are only an assumption; there are no true zeros, and there are no units of measurement. This latter characteristic means that what psychometric tests measure is uncertain and evidence of their validity is required. In fact good psychometric tests have their own conventions. They have to be shown to be reliable, valid and to have good norms, this to make their scores interpretable in the absence of a true zero. In this Primer we have demonstrated that there are a number of tests, particularly in the field of ability but also in the field of personality, which meet rigorous psychometric criteria and which have been shown to be effective in applied psychology and in the development of psychological theory. Cattell's Comprehensive Ability Battery (Hakstian and Cattell, 1976) and the Eysenck Personality Questionnaire (Eysenck and Eysenck, 1975) are two such tests. Finally, it was noted in our study of tests that Rasch scaling (Rasch, 1960) was an approach to test construction which was claimed by its enthusiasts to be measurement in the scientific sense. However, it was pointed out that even though (provided items can be found to fit the model) equal interval scaling can be achieved there are no clear units of measurement. Rasch scales have underlying latent traits which, by definition, cannot be known. They do not seem therefore to be suited to scientific measurement.

Michell (1997) argued that to believe, as psychologists do, that psychometrics is scientific measurement is a form of mass delusion, which he traces back to the work of Stevens on psychological scaling (Stevens, 1946). There he argued that many of the measurement problems can be avoided by operationally defining variables. Thus intelligence is what intelligence tests measure. Although this passed into general psychology, almost without comment, as Michell (1997) shows, in fact it is incoherent with the realist viewpoint implicit in science.

As is made clear throughout this Primer, current psychometrics is not worthless. It has provided good quality measurement, when its techniques are properly used and the work on intelligence, both theoretical and applied, demonstrates this point well (for example, Jensen, 1998). On the other hand, it is difficult to see how to progress. To take the case of the g factor, despite its power in explanation and in prediction, we still do not understand the nature of intelligence. To define it as reasoning power is too vague and general. Similarly in other fields of measurement we have no clear notion of the nature of extraversion and anxiety. It is not sufficient, for the science of psychology, to know that extraverts make good sales personnel or lose concentration more easily than introverts (Eysenck, 1967). These observations require precise explanation.

In the light of these difficulties and the arguments of Michell (1990, 1997) and the powerful but complex work of Luce and Tukey (1964) and their colleagues in mathematical psychology, I attempted to draw up a blueprint for a new approach to psychometrics. The aim was to produce scientific psychometric tests – ratio scales with clear, unequivocal units of measurement.

In this way, it was hoped, psychometrics could advance into the Millennium and become a true natural science.

In *The New Psychometrics* (Kline, 1998) I set out some possible approaches to this task, which, it has to be said, have been greeted with considerable scepticism by many psychometrists. In this final chapter I want to describe, briefly and simply, how such a New Psychometrics might be developed, because I believe that this must be the way forward. It may prove impossible, and it is certainly difficult, but the rewards are huge – a psychology based upon precise quantification, a true natural science.

The BIP

The BIP, according to the Erlangen school of psychology (for example, Lehrl and Fischer, 1990), is the basic period of information processing. This BIP is a basic psychological parameter, a physiological and general determinant of intelligence which is measurable at the ratio level and which correlates with the WAIS (see Chapter 5), –.60. Furthermore the BIP involves bits as the units of information. In other words the BIP is precisely what is required for the New Psychometrics, a true derived ratio measure with a clear unit of measurement. Thus the definition of the BIP is the shortest possible time during which a person can process one bit of information.

Rationale and Measurement of the BIP

The measurement of the BIP, which turns out to be remarkably simple, is rooted in its theoretical rationale – the sequential, binary model of information processing postulated by Frank (1969). This asserts that each bit of information to be processed requires a separate step: one bit, one step, three bits, three steps and so on. However, processing demands are determined not by the stimuli but by the expectations of subjects. Thus if a subject had to recognise 'a' from a list of vowels, the information content of the stimulus is 2.32 bits since $5 = 2^{2.32}$. However, if 'a' were from a list of English letters then the information content would be 4.70 bits since $26 = 2^{4.70}$. There are other parameters in this model which should be briefly mentioned. For example, it is claimed that information bombards us so quickly that it is beyond the capacity of the brain to process it so that it has to be filtered to accommodate what is important. This accommodation rate is claimed to be 15 bits/second for the average adult. This, by definition, is clearly similar to the BIP and is held to represent the information flow to working memory. This is known as C_k. This filtered information resides for a finite time in working memory – T_r. The final parameter is K_k, the total capacity of working memory which is estimated from the product of C_k and T_r.

Measurement of the BIP and other Parameters

C_k is measured thus. Subjects have to read 20 letters as quickly as possible. As argued, such an array has an informational content of 100 bits (rounding 4.7 to 5 since humans make only whole binary decisions). Thus the time (t) to read the card = the processing time for 100 bits; $C_k = 100/t$, and the BIP is, therefore, the reciprocal of C_k. However, the Erlangen school prefers to use the BIP simply because it is more related to basic information processing and to physiology. T_t is measured with the digit span test, part of the Wechsler scales (see Chapter 5) and $K_k = C_k \times T_t$.

Comments on the BIP

There are several points that need to be made about the BIP because it exemplifies so clearly what will be involved in the development of the new psychometrics, regardless as to whether it turns out to provide a ratio measure of intelligence.

- The BIP, defined as the shortest possible time to process 1 bit of information, must be a genuine ratio scale. There is a true zero, there are equal intervals and a unit of measurement which is quite unequivocal. Furthermore this measure has real psychological meaning (processing speed) which must be universal across all informational processing organisms and, from the viewpoint of the measurement of human ability, must be in addition culture- and attainment-free.
- The measure is embedded in cognitive psychological theory – that of Frank (1969). This is important and in contrast with the empiricism of conventional psychometrics where, as has been shown, there is always the problem of identifying factors and latent traits. It is to be noted that this is a general point. It is not asserting that this particular theory is correct.
- The necessity for good cognitive theories. Obviously if there are no theories, and this is almost the case in the field of personality, such that clear guidelines for fundamental measurement are present or can be deduced, there are difficulties. This may be true of Frank's theory in that it assumes reading the alphabet necessitates a sequential and binary process and if this is not the case the measurements are bound to be in error.

Summary of Findings with the BIP

Kline et al. (1994), Draycott and Kline (1994a) and Draycott (1996) decided to investigate the BIP in order to study the claims of the Erlangen school in a number of studies. We attempted to locate the BIP in factor space using the best measures of ability, the Comprehensive Ability Battery, AH6, Raven's Matrices and the Mill–Hill Vocabulary scale which were all described in Chapter 5, and the clearest test of personality, the EPQ, which was described in Chapter 6, in a simple structure, rotated factor analysis (see Chapter 4). Here I shall summarise the results of all these studies together, and for further details readers can consult the references above or Kline (1998).

- In the study with Raven's matrices, the BIP loaded both the crystallised and the fluid ability factors. However, the correlations with the intelligence scales were far lower than that reported in the original Erlangen studies. The BIP correlated only .216 with Raven's matrices, which is one of the best measures of fluid intelligence. This is disappointing because any biological measure of intelligence ought to correlate most highly with measures of fluid intelligence.
- In the study with the AH6, with 106 subjects, the previous findings and those of the Erlangen school were not replicated. A three-factor solution yielded a general intelligence factor, a personality factor and a third factor loading C_k and T_r. When we included an attainment factor, based on examination results, in the analysis, the BIP failed to load the g factors but loaded an attainment factor on which the crystallised ability scale from AH6 also loaded. This was surprising and this is discussed later in this section.
- In the study with the CAB the BIP correlated positively with the V scale, verbal ability, which is salient to crystallised intelligence. This could be interpreted as evidence that reading speed, which is the basis of the BIP, reflects how much a person has read. In the rotated factor analysis the BIP loaded the crystallised intelligence factor. It should be noted that K_k, the total capacity of short-term memory, when put separately into the factor analysis (without the BIP) also loaded this crystallised intelligence factor.
- Conclusions. These studies clearly demonstrate that the BIP correlates with crystallised rather than fluid ability. This would account for the correlation with the WAIS but does not support its interpretation as a measure of basic processing speed. The loadings on crystallised intelligence and the correlation with verbal ability suggest that it is more simply interpreted as a measure of reading speed, which is a recognised primary ability factor. This is supported in similar findings by Roberts et al. (1996) and Vigil-Colet et al. (1997).
- Concluding comments on the BIP. The BIP, contrary to the claims of Lehrl and Fischer (1990), does not measure fluid ability and thus is unlikely to be a measure of processing speed. However, it could be

argued that the intelligence test scores themselves are too influenced by learning and experience to be suitable as criteria for the BIP, although this is somewhat implausible. It could further be argued that the fault lay in Frank's cognitive model and this is possible, but the most simple explanation, that the BIP is really a measure of reading speed, is the most likely of the findings. Nevertheless, despite this the BIP illustrates the approach to measurement, embedded in psychological cognitive theorising, which the New Psychometrics must take.

Other Possible Fundamental Measures of Intelligence and Ability

There have been a number of attempts to investigate the nature of g using the notion of the elementary cognitive process which is an integral part of cognitive psychology. These have been fully described and discussed in Kline (1998) and Carroll (1993). The point of this work was not to yield fundamental measures but to explicate the nature of human abilities, although often reaction times were used which are, of course, extensive ratio scales. Some of these tests do correlate with intelligence positively and reliably but at a rather low level so that at best they are only indicants of how a New Psychometrics might look, a basis from which to begin. Here, because of their tentative nature as new psychometric measures a brief summary will be sufficient.

Elementary Cognitive Tasks (ECTs)

Carroll (1993) has surveyed ECTs and shows that ten varieties of cognitive task are most frequently investigated. Reaction times, for example, touching a lever if a red light glows, can be broken down into decision times and movement times with most experimental apparatus. There are various varieties of reaction time task: simple reaction time to a stimulus; choice reaction time where there are several possible stimuli; categorisation reaction time, for example R for red lever; odd-man reaction time where subjects have to respond to the most distant of three stimuli. Then there are the Posner (1978) tasks where subjects have to decide whether two stimuli are the same or different; visual search where the presence or absence of stimuli in a list has to be indicated; scan and search similar to the above; memory search in which a set of stimuli having been presented, one stimulus is shown and subjects have to indicate whether it was in the list or not; inspection time – the time necessary to determine the difference between two stimuli, auditory or visual; and sentence verification – the time taken to show whether a sentence correctly describes, for example, a visual pattern.

Comments on ECTs

The relevance of these ECTs to the New Psychometrics is that they are claimed to measure elementary cognitive processes which, as has been argued in the case of the BIP, is a necessary part of the procedure. In addition, most of these are reaction times which are ratio measures in the full sense of the term.

However, examination of the cognitive literature, for example Sternberg (1969) or Baddeley (1999), indicates that the identification of the cognitive mechanisms underlying these ECTs is speculative. Workers in the field tend to assume that the underlying claims, which sound reasonable, are true. This is a problem for the New Psychometrics since it is therefore necessary to identify empirically what these ECTs do measure and the obvious solution, as Carroll (1993) points out, is factor analysis, either of the ECTs alone or perhaps even more efficient factor analysis of ECTs and ability factors. An ideal result, from the viewpoint of the New Psychometrics, would be the discovery of one of these measures or a combination of them, all ratio scales, which predicted real life behaviour as well as or better than g.

Before I summarise the results of such factor analyses, there is one further point discussed by Carroll (1993). Some of these ECTs may be little different from the primary ability factors discussed in Chapter 5, as indeed was the case with the BIP. In fact Carroll points out that three of these ECTs resemble the perceptual speed factor – inspection time and the two search tasks. Indeed these ECTs are tests for the factor.

Factor Analyses of the ECTs

Unfortunately, as Carroll (1993) argues, the factor analysis of ECTs is far from simple. Thus these can vary in terms of stimuli and experimental conditions which makes comparisons difficult and, in addition, many ECTs are of low reliability because they are essentially one item tests (see Chapter 3).

The Work of Kranzler (1990)

As Carroll (1993) demonstrates, one of the best factor analytic studies of ECTs is that of Kranzler (1990) and I shall summarise the most important of his findings. In the first-order analyses decision times appear on different factors depending on the ECT from which they were derived. This suggests that there is considerable specific variance in ECTs. The mean and standard deviations of these decision times also loaded the same factors.

However, the two second-order factors are of particular relevance. One loaded on the movement-time factors and was independent of psychometric variables, demonstrating that movement times are not a measure of ability. However, the second factor loaded decision times and psychometric measures of ability, both crystallised and fluid. This suggests that these ECTs do measure abilities, although it should be noted that they loaded the factor more highly than the psychometric measures of intelligence. This research is unable to determine whether this second-order factor is a good measure of intelligence and it is necessary to see whether these ECTs in some combination can predict real-life criteria. If they were as good or better than intelligence tests we would be on the way to developing an extensive measure of human ability – a derived measure.

As we have argued these ECTs are held to represent various processing component stages in problem solving: the response component; decision component; encoding component; and comparison component. Some tasks require one of these stages, others many or all of them. Kyllonen (1985) computed from ECTs, requiring more or fewer components, times for these different components and factor analysed the results. Six factors emerged but these were highly correlated and there were different factors associated with letter-matching and word matching tasks which suggest that they are somewhat specific. Indeed the factor analysis could be held to demonstrate that there is essentially a cognitive speed factor accounting for the results. Indeed Carroll (1993) has argued that speed may account for the relationship of ECTs and intelligence since intelligence tests are speeded.

Roberts (1997) carried out a detailed study of ECTs and psychometric ability which took into account the points raised by Carroll (1993). Eleven ECTs were factored in the first part of the study and at the third order there was a general factor of response speed, chronometric t, which supports the claims in the previous paragraph. At the second order, there were two factors – movement time and decision time.

In the second part of the study these factors were correlated with psychometric tests of ability. Fluid intelligence correlated about .4 with decision time and chronometric t. Crystallised intelligence correlated only with the first-order factor decision time to verbal codes, while perceptual speed correlated .6 with chronometric t and beyond .4 with movement time and decision time. ECTs would appear to measure speed.

Conclusions Concerning ECTs

In general there are no clear findings. ECTs have not been demonstrated to measure intelligence although they correlate with intelligence tests. However, this may be a function of speed and it would appear that ECTs essentially measure speed.

Speed and Intelligence

Clearly if ECTs are to be considered as possible fundamental measures of ability, it is necessary to investigate the link between speed and intelligence and I shall now briefly describe an attempt do this by Draycott (1996) and Draycott and Kline (1994b, 1996). In these studies the CAB (Hakstian and Cattell, 1976), which has been described in this Primer and is a good measure of the primary ability factors, together with the AGARD tests (Reeves et al., 1991), a series of ECTs, were subjected to a simple structure, oblique, rotated factor analysis, having been administered to 113 subjects. The AGARD ECTs are claimed to measure the most important cognitive processes and include measures of reaction time, mathematical processing, memory search, spatial processing, tracking, grammatical reasoning (to measure working memory) and dual task performance. Each of these tasks, other than the tracking, yields separate measures of speed and accuracy.

Surprisingly the results were clear-cut. There was a speed factor loading all the AGARD speed measures. Only one ability test, speed of closure, loaded this factor. Fluid intelligence was the second factor and only the AGARD mathematical processing ECT loaded this. Factor 3 was the tracking factor and factor 4 loaded crystallised ability.

It can be concluded that speed and intelligence are separate. There is a separate cognitive speed factor and for this reason these results suggest that ECTs are unlikely to form the basis of scientific measures of ability despite the fact that they yield ratio scales. This cognitive speed factor was further investigated (Draycott and Kline, 1994b) with school students where it was shown that it could not predict performance in GCSE examinations. With a small sample of university students (Draycott, 1996) the AGARD score did load the academic performance factor, presumably because in these exams writing a lot is an advantage (the prolixity of academia). However, the speed factor was also confounded with measures of personality and this adds a further unwanted complication if ECTs are to be used as fundamental measures of ability.

Reaction Time and Inspection Time

These are two ECTs which have been subjected to so much investigation in relation to intelligence that a little more needs to be said about them.

I shall begin with reaction time. The relation of reaction time and intelligence has been extensively studied by Jensen (1987a, b), Barrett et al. (1989) and Vernon (1987), the rationale being that intelligence depends on rapid information processing of which reaction times are a good measure. Indeed Hick's law (Hick, 1952) states that reaction times increase as a linear function of the number of choices which supports such a rationale. Unfortunately, however, Barrett et al. (1989) showed that about 30% of subjects did not fit Hick's law which destroys the theoretical basis of using reaction time as a measure of abilities. Even so it is interesting that the correlation between intelligence and the standard deviation of reaction times is .48 (as distinct from the correlation of .2 with the mean). However, such findings make it doubtful if reaction times will be ultimately useful in the quest for extensive measure of human abilities. The use of standard deviations, it should be noted, is based upon the notion of processing efficiency, less variance being expected in efficient systems.

Inspection time, the time taken reliably to discriminate two lines of different length, briefly exposed in a tachistoscope, was at one time regarded as a possible panacea to many of the problems of intelligence testing, eliminating, as it did, the influences of education, social class and educational opportunities. This was a measure of mental speed. Brand and Deary (1982), summarising a number of small-scale studies in Edinburgh, concluded that the correlation between IT and Ravens matrices was –.72. However, I believe this to be a huge overestimate, perhaps due to psychometric problems of sampling and very small numbers of subjects, on occasion as few as six, a point also made by Mackintosh (1986).

Deary and Stough (1996) in a survey of all studies to that date, admit that the correlation was far smaller, around .3, but argue that that it is highly consistent. However, with the correlation as low as this several points need to be made. First, it is clear that, as it stands, despite its ratio scaling IT could not be substituted for an intelligence test. Furthermore a study by Cooper et al. (1986) in which the IT was correlated with the main primary ability factors (although in only a small sample) showed its highest correlation was with the factor of perceptual speed. This makes sense especially since Roberts (1997), in a study already reported, found that IT loaded on the speed factor chronometric *t*. There is one final point: Barrett (1999) showed that in his studies of intelligence and inspection time, there were far too many subjects of high intelligence and slow IT and vice versa to be able to make any kind of causal deterministic claims about the nature of the relationship between IT and intelligence. Similar arguments are likely to apply to a newly developed measure of mental speed, the Frequency Accrual Speed Test (FAST) (Vickers et al., 1995), where subjects have to discriminate relative frequency of stimuli.

Conclusions

Despite the research on the relationship between intelligence and reaction times and inspection times, it is unlikely that these will turn out to be useful in the measurement of human abilities, being rather a measure of mental speed, which all recent research shows to be only modestly correlated with intelligence, a gloomy view supported by Stankov et al. (1995) and Jensen (1998).

Physiological Indices

Jensen (1998), in his detailed study of the meaning of g, comes to a conclusion not unlike the one advocated in this Primer, although he was not writing from the perspective of the New Psychometrics. There he argued that although intelligence tests were reliable and valid and were able to predict well in a variety of situations, if more knowledge was to be gained concerning the nature of intelligence, then we have to turn to physiology. Although reductionism can be misused in psychology, there can be no doubt that a full knowledge requires a proper understanding of the underlying physiology. This is so self-evident that it should need no argument. For example, it would be possible to demonstrate that eyes had greater acuity in bright light than in dull with no knowledge of rods, cones or foveas. Few psychologists would, however, support the notion that the physiology was irrelevant.

From the viewpoint of fundamental, extensive measurement, in principle the measurement of the relevant physiological indices would be excellent. Indeed, as I have argued (1998) and in this Primer, this is where I believe the future of psychometrics must lie – in precise measurement of the underlying physiology, and not only of course as regards human abilities, but also in the field of personality and motivation.

At this point I have to admit that, as yet, there are no such physiological measures of either ability or personality, although some work has begun. For this reason and because this is a Psychometrics Primer, in this brief section I shall simply indicate the way this new research is developing. For more detail readers should consult Kline (1998) or Jensen (1997, 1998).

Physiological Indices of Ability

Jensen (1997) makes two crucial methodological points which must be discussed. The first deals with his approach to studying the correlations between physical variables and human abilities – correlated vectors. A vector (a column of numbers) is formed from the g loadings of the ability tests. A second vector is formed from the correlation of these tests with the physical variable (for example, brain size). Then after allowing for the influence of reliabilities the correlation between these vectors is computed. This indicates not the size of the correlation of individual differences in g with the physical variable but the fact that there is a relationship at all. The size of this relationship must be computed from the factor scores on g and the scores on the physical variable.

In addition Jensen (1997) draws a distinction between intrinsic and incidental correlations. Intrinsic correlations can be observed within families, that is, the differences between siblings on IQ are correlated with their differences on a physical variable. Such correlations do not always occur. Often correlations between variables are found only between families (incidental correlations) and Jensen shows that it makes sense to investigate as possible physiological bases of intelligence only those physical variables where intrinsic correlations with IQ can be observed.

Physical Variables Showing Intrinsic Correlations with g

Jensen (1997) lists the following variables: myopia; brain and head size; glucose metabolic rate; reaction time; averaged evoked potential; and nerve conduction velocity. The correlation with myopia is small, .25, and this alone would make it worthless for our purposes as a possible extensive measure of intelligence. It is an example of pleiotropy where different traits are influenced by the same genes.

It is assumed that head size reflects brain size (even though the correlation is only about .5) and this is what gives some meaning to the correlation with g. According to Jensen (1994) the g loading of a test is a good predictor of its correlation with head size. However, based upon meta-analyses of studies of brain size conducted using magnetic resonance imaging, the correlation with intelligence or cognitive ability, ranging from .36 to .44 (Rushton and Ankney (1996), is far too small to make it useful as an extensive measure of intelligence.

The glucose metabolic rate (GMR) is, perhaps, the most promising of these physiological indices. GMR is measured by PET scan which monitors the uptake of radioactive glucose in various parts of the brain as problems are solved, the rationale being that glucose is the main fuel of brain metabolism. Haier (1993) has been responsible for much of the research in this area in which the results are highly complex. Thus although GMR increases within individuals as problems get harder, high IQ subjects have a lower GMR for the same problem than do low IQ subjects, with complex interactions between ability level and task difficulty. High IQ subjects show greater localisation of GMR than those of lower ability and practise decreases GMR. Finally there is the interesting finding that, when using the method of correlated vectors applied to the WAIS, there is a high correlation between g loading and its correlation with the GMR. GMR, therefore, may be an index of brain efficiency. It is important to improve the precision of measurement of GMR and it is possible that this could become useful in the development of extensive measures of human ability.

We have fully discussed the use of reaction times as possible indices of intelligence. There are small but consistent correlations between intelligence and the means and variances of reaction times but this is all. Any adequate theory of intelligence must be able to accommodate this fact.

The correlation between intelligence and the averaged evoked potential (AEP), sometimes referred to as event related potential (ERP), which are EEG measurements in response to stimuli, has been the subject of enormous amounts of research. However, although some spectacular findings have been claimed, both these and more modest findings have proven virtually impossible to replicate, as careful surveys of the literature by Barrett and Eysenck (1992) and Deary and Caryl (1993) have made clear. On occasions, indeed, these authors found that it was not a case of failure to replicate but of actual reversal. This makes dubious some of the recent spectacular claims concerning the nature of intelligence, based on EEG studies, by Robinson (for example, 1999).

If EEG measures do reflect brain activity, that there are correlations with problem solving is actually not of enormous interest. Indeed what is required to make EEG studies of real scientific value is two-fold. First, there must be huge improvements in the precision of EEG measurement. It must be absolutely clear what each EEG output is measuring. Second, it must be specified from a theoretical account of intelligence what electrical activity is to be expected. If these conditions could be met by EEG studies then AEPs and other EEG measures (such as P300 latencies which are faster in high intelligence subjects than lower) might well turn out to be useful. However, at present it must be argued that EEG is not a viable index of ability, a viewpoint supported by Brody (1992) who considers that even the hope of using the ERP as a measure of intelligence is vain, and by Stelmack and Houlihan (1995) who accept the fact that EEG gives an incomplete picture of brain activity.

Finally mention must be made of nerve conduction velocity, NRV. It might be assumed that the faster this was the better. What studies have been done are contradictory for no obvious reasons as Jensen (1997) argues. Indeed, the highest correlation observed with fluid intelligence is only .27 and this is by no means sufficient as a base for an extensive measure of intelligence.

Jensen (1997) discusses one further physiological basis to intelligence. Miller (1994) proposed that individual differences in intelligence might be related to the degree of myelination in the axons of the brain. This paper was based upon a careful survey of relevant papers but lacks the clear physiological evidence required to support it. In principle the necessary research is simple.

Conclusions

As was suggested at the beginning of this section, at present no adequate physiologically extensive measures have been developed. However, this is undoubtedly the next task for psychometrics and as the technology improves it is possible, as has been seen, that real advances will be made.

Physiological Indices of Personality

My discussion of possible physiological measures of personality will be very brief. This is because the physiology of personality is even less well developed than that of human abilities, as was made clear in Chapter 6. Eysenck (1967a) is the only researcher to have any coherent approach to the underlying physiology of personality factors and he has argued that extraversion reflects the arousability of the central nervous system and neuroticism the lability of the autonomic nervous system, while psychoticism reflects the androgen level of the individual.

Thus measures of the arousability of the CNS and the lability of the ANS ought to be excellent bases for the development of fundamental, extensive measures of the largest personality factors, extraversion and neuroticism.

I shall deal with neuroticism first. Fahrenberg (1992) carried out a brilliant and devastating survey of the studies of the psychophysiology of neuroticism, a field notorious for confused and contradictory results. He demonstrated beyond doubt that the notion of arousability was empty. There was no such general concept. Thus he shows that different indices of the same physiological construct do not necessarily correlate – what is referred to as response fractionation. This, of course, applies not only to the lability of the ANS but also to the arousal of the CNS which is relevant to scientific measures of extraversion. Thus this not only means that any physiological index will be unsatisfactory as a measure of personality but it also casts doubt on the meaning of arousal, which would appear to be an empty concept. Thus he concludes that any single measurements of heart rate, EEG or electrodermal activity are incoherent with physiology. Something different is required. There must be a better, more precise physiological basis for neuroticism which does not depend on concepts which cannot be supported.

As has been indicated, the strictures of Fahrenberg concerning the generality of broad concepts of arousal apply to extraversion with equal force. Thus it is necessary to seek physiological indices which have high correlations with extraversion. That they have means that response fractionation is not a problem. Stelmack and Geen (1992) have a succinct and rigorous review of the research in this field. As measures of arousal, skin conductance level (SCL) has been measured in extraverts and introverts, the latter being supposedly highly aroused. Findings are confused and contradictory and it is evident that SCL will not do as a scientific measure. The same is true of the skin conductance response to stimulation (SCR) where reversed results occur with more intense stimuli and selection of subjects appears to be critical. Clearly SCR would not be useful for a scientific measure.

Similarly, other physiological indices such as cardiovascular activity, systolic blood pressure and biochemical activity fail to yield correlations with extraversion. In the case of ERPs to auditory stimuli, although there is some consistency in the results of introverts and extraverts, the measures are unlikely to be useful because they are affected by different experimental conditions. Again it must be concluded that no current physiological indices are suitable as measures of extraversion. What is required is a sounder physiological basis for the factor and, better, more precise physiological indices.

Conclusions

It is quite clear what needs to be done in the New Psychometrics, both in respect of ability and personality. The main factors in both fields, as revealed by current psychometrics, must not be abandoned. These need to be studied afresh so that a new, more precise physiological basis can be set up. This ought to yield more adequate physiological indices as a basis for fundamental measurement.

In the case of human intelligence, far more attention needs to be paid to current cognitive psychology so that a more precise account of the mental processing can be developed. From this it is possible that fundamental measures may be developed.

Thus there is much innovative research and thinking required. This will be the basis of the New Psychometrics, for the current psychometrics has come about as far as it can. It is efficient in practice and far superior to intuitive procedures and until the New Psychometrics is developed it must continue, properly done, as set out in this Primer.

However, it is possible that the optimism of the New Psychometrics is unfounded. It could be that it is not possible to develop extensive measures of intelligence or personality. If that is so then this harsh truth has to be faced. Psychometrics cannot become a true science. The current psychometrics can be slowly (albeit minimally) improved and can continue to function as a powerful set of pragmatic procedures useful in selection or in the clinic. However, it will not lead to the wonderful increases in knowledge which have characterised the natural sciences. And it is for this reason that the hard graft of the New Psychometrics is worthwhile. It is not for the faint of heart.

Glossary

Alpha coefficient   The best index of the internal consistency reliability of a test. The formula is: $r_{kk} = k/k-1 (1-\Sigma\sigma^2_i\sqrt{\sigma^2_y})$ where r_{kk} = the alpha coefficient of a test of k items, k = the number of items, σ^2 = the item variance, σ^2_y = the variance of the test and Σ = the sum of (as used in subsequent formulae).

Correction of attenuation due to low reliability   Correlations are reduced by the imperfect reliability of the variables. A correction formula is sometimes applied: $r(\text{corrected}) = r_{12} / \sqrt{r_{11}\sqrt{r_{22}}}$ where r_2 is the obtained correlation, r_{11} is the reliability of test 1 and r_{22} is the reliability of test 2.

Correlation coefficient (r)   An index of the degree of relationship between two variables. The index runs from +1, perfect agreement, to –1, perfect disagreement. A correlation of .000 indicates that there is no relationship at all. The formula is: $r = N\Sigma XY - \Sigma X\Sigma Y/\sqrt{N\Sigma X^2 - (\Sigma X)^2}\sqrt{N\Sigma Y^2 - (\Sigma Y)^2}$ where X and Y are the variables and N is the number in the sample.

Covariance   The average cross-product of two sets of deviation scores. The formula is: $\sigma_{12} = \Sigma x_1x_2/N$ where σ_{12} = the covariance, x_1 = a deviation score on variable 1, x_2 = a deviation score on variable 2 and N = number of subjects.

Delta, δ   This is an index of the distribution of a set of scores. A rectangular distribution yields a delta of 1.00. The normal distribution has a delta of .93. The higher the delta, the greater the discriminatory power of the test. The formula is: $\delta = (n + 1)(N^2 - \Sigma f^2_1)$ where N = number of subjects, n = number of items and f_1 = the frequency at each score.

Factor   Any linear combination of variables can constitute a factor. Factors can be conceived as constructs or dimensions, vectors which can account for the correlations in a correlation matrix.

Factor loadings   These are the correlations of the variables with the factors or the weights for predicting the factors. In orthogonal rotations and unrotated factor analyses these are identical.

Oblique rotations of factors   These rotate factors to the oblique position, the cosine of the angle between the factors being the correlation between them. The oblique factor structure matrix indicates the correlations of the variables with the factors and the factor pattern matrix shows the weights for predicting the factors.

Orthogonal rotation of factors   Here the factors are rotated so that the factors are at right angles to each other and are uncorrelated.

Mean   The average of a set of scores. The formula is: mean $= \Sigma X/N$ where X is a score on the test and $N =$ the number of subjects.

Multiple regression   The statistical technique to compute the correlation between a set of scores and some criterion score.

Normal Curve   This is the bell-shaped Gaussian curve with mathematical properties highly useful in parametric statistics.

Standard deviation   This is an index of the variability of a set of scores. The formula is: $\sigma = \sqrt{\text{variance}}$ where $\sigma =$ the standard deviation.

Standard error of measurement   This is the range of scores, given the obtained score, within which the true score falls, at various degrees of probability. The formula is: $\sigma_{meas} = \sigma x \sqrt{1 - r_{xx}}$ where $\sigma_x =$ the standard deviation of test x and $r_{xx} =$ the reliability of test x.

Standard scores   Sets of scores transformed to have new means and standard deviations. Standard scores of the same type are directly comparable. Some commonly used standard scores are: T scores (mean 50, standard deviation 10); standard scores (mean zero, standard deviation 1). All these standard scores can be in normalised form, if required. The formula is: $X_t = \sigma_t/\sigma_o (X_o - M_o) = M_t$ where $X_t =$ score on transformed scale, $X_o =$ score on original scale, $M_o =$ mean of original scale, $M_t =$ mean of transformed scale, σ_o = standard deviation of original scale and σ_t = standard deviation of transformed scale.

True score This is the hypothetical score a subject would have obtained if he or she had taken all the items in the relevant universe of items from which it is assumed that the test items are a random sample.

Variance An index of the variability of a set of scores around their mean. The formula is: $\sigma^2 = \Sigma\, x^2/N$ where σ^2 = the variance, x = the deviation of a score from the mean and N = the number of measurements.

Bibliography

Adorno, T.W., Frenkel-Brunswick, E., Levinson, D.J. and Sandford, R.N. (1950). *The Authoritarian Personality*. New York, Harper & Row.

Allport, G.W. (1937). *Personality: A Psychological Interpretation*. New York, Holt, Rinehart & Winston.

American Psychiatric Association (1994). *Diagnostic and Statistical Manual of Mental Disorders*. Washington, American Psychiatric Association.

Angleitner, J. and Wiggins, J.S. (eds) (1988). *Personality Assessment via Questionnaires*. Berlin, Springer-Verlag.

Baddeley, A. (1990). *Human Memory: Theory and Practice*. Hillsdale, Erlbaum.

Baddeley, A, (1999). *Essentials of Human Memory*. Hove, Psychology Press.

Barrett, P. (1998). Rasch Scaling: yet another incomprehensible test theory or something far more dangerous? Paper presented at Conference of Occupational Psychology, Birkbeck College.

Barrett, P. (1999). Individual Differences: the end of an era. Where do we go from here? Paper presented at Conference of Occupational Psychology, Birkbeck College.

Barrett, P. and Eysenck, H.J. (1992). Brain electrical potentials and intelligence. In Gale, A. and Eysenck, M.W. (eds) (1992).

Barrett, P. and Kline, P. (1981a). A comparison between Rasch analysis and factor analysis of items in the EPQ. *Journal of Personality and Group Behaviour*, **1**, 1–22.

Barrett, P. and Kline, P. (1981b). The observation to variable ratio in factor analyses. *Journal of Personality and Group Behaviour*, **1**, 23–33.

Barrett, P. and Kline, P. (1982). The itemetric properties of the Eysenck Personality Questionnaire: a reply to Helmes. *Personality and Individual Differences*, **3**, 73–80.

Barrett, P., Eysenck, H.J. and Luching, S. (1989). Reaction time and intelligence: a replicated study. *Intelligence*, **10**, 9–40.

Barrett, P., Kline, P., Paltiel, L. and Eysenck, H.J. (1996). An evaluation of the psychometric properties of the Concept 5.2. Personality Questionnaire. *Journal of Occupational and Organisational Psychology*, **69**, 1–19.

Barrick, M.R. and Mount, M.K. (1991). The big five personality dimensions and job performance: a meta-analysis. *Personnel Psychology*, **44**, 1–26.

Barton, K.S. and Cattell, R.B. (1981). *The Central State–Trait Kit (CTS): Experimental Version*. Champaign, IPAT.

Bartram, D., Anderson, N., Kellett, D., Lindley, P. and Robertson, I. (eds) (1995). *Review of Personality Assessment Instruments (level B) for Use in Occupational Settings*. Leicester, BPS Books.

Bartram, D., Lindley, J., Foster, J. and Marshall, L. (eds) (1992). *Review of Psychometric Tests (level A) for Assessment in Vocational Training.* Leicester, BPS Books.

Beck, A.T. (1962). Reliability of psychiatric diagnoses: a critique of systematic studies. *American Journal of Psychiatry,* **119**, 210–215.

Beck, S.J. (1944). *Rorschach's Test. Vol. 1: Basic Processes.* New York, Grune and Stratton.

Bendig, A.W. (1959). Score reliability of dichotomous and trichotomous item responses in the MPI. *Journal of Consulting and Clinical Psychology,* **23**, 181–185.

Binet, A. and Simon, T. (1905). Methodes nouvelles pour le diagnostic du niveau intellectual des anormaux. *L'Annee Psychologique,* **11**, 191–244.

Blinkhorn, S.E. (1998). Past imperfect, future conditional: fifty years of test theory. *British Journal of Mathematical and Statistical Psychology,* **50**, 175–185.

Block, J. (1995). A contrarian view of the five factor approach to personality description. *Psychological Bulletin,* **117**, 187–225.

Bolton, B.F. (1986). Clinical diagnosis and psychotherapeutic monitoring. In Cattell, R.B. and Johnson, R.C. (1986).

Boring, E.G. (1923). Intelligence as the tests test it. *New Republic,* **35**, 35–37.

Boyle, G.J. and Katz, I. (1991). Multidimensional scaling of the Eight-State Questionnaire and the Differential Emotions Scale. *Personality and Individual Differences,* **12**, 565–574.

Boyle, G.J., Stankov, L. and Cattell, R.B. (1995). Measurement and statistical models in the study of personality and intelligence. In Saklofske, D.H. and Zeidner, M. (eds) (1995).

Braden, J.P. (1995). Intelligence and personality in school and educational psychology. In Saklofske, D.H, and Zeidner, M. (eds) (1995).

Brand, C.R. and Deary, I.J. (1982). Intelligence and inspection time. In Eysenck, H.J. (ed.) (1982).

Brody, N. (1992) *Intelligence.* San Diego, Academic Press.

Brody, N. and Crowley, M.J. (1995). Environmental (and genetic) influences on personality and intelligence. In Saklofske, D.H. and Zeidner, M. (eds) (1995)

Buck, J.N. (1948). Manual for the HTP. *Monograph Supplement 5, Journal of Clinical Psychology.*

Buck, (1970). *The House Tree Person Technique: Revised Manual.* Los Angeles, Western Psychological Services.

Buros, O.K. (ed.) (1959). *The VIth Mental Measurement Yearbook.* Highland Park, Gryphon Press.

Buros, O.K. (ed.) (1972) *The VIIth Mental Measurement Yearbook.* Highland Park, Gryphon Press.

Burr, V. (1995). *An Introduction to Social Constructionism.* London, Routledge.

Burt, C.L. (1940). *The Factors of the Mind.* London, University of London Press.

Butcher, J.N. (1990). *MMPI-2 in Psychological Treatment.* New York, Oxford University Press.

Carroll, J.B. (1993). *Human Cognitive Abilities.* Cambridge, Cambridge University Press.

Carstairs, G.M. (1957). *The Twice-Born: A Study of a Community of High Caste Hindus.* London, Hogarth Press.

Cattell, R.B. (1957). *Personality and Motivation Structure and Measurement.* Yonkers, World Book Co.

Cattell, R.B. (1971). *Abilities: their Structure Growth and Action.* New York, Brunner Mazel.

Cattell, R.B. (1973). *Personality and Mood by Questionnaire.* San-Francisco, Jossey-Bass.

Cattell, R.B. (1978). *The Scientific Use of Factor Analysis*. New York, Plenum.

Cattell, R.B. (1981). *Personality and Learning Theory*. New York, Springer.

Cattell, R.B. (1985). *Human Motivation and the Dynamic Calculus*. New York, Praeger.

Cattell, R.B. and Butcher, H.J. (1968). *The Prediction of Academic Achievement*. Indianapolis, Bobbs-Merrill.

Cattell, R.B. and Cattell, A.K.S. (1959). *The Culture Fair Test*. Champaign, IPAT.

Cattell, R.B. and Child, D. (1975). *Motivation and Dynamic Structure*. London, Holt, Rinehart and Winston.

Cattell, R.B. and Johnson, R.C. (eds) (1986). *Functional Psychological Testing*. New York, Brunner Mazel.

Cattell, R.B. and Kline, P. (1977). *The Scientific Analysis of Personality and Motivation*. London, Academic Press.

Cattell, R.B. and Schuerger, J. (1978). *Personality Theory in Action: Handbook for the Objective–Analytic (O–A) Test Kit*. Champaign, IPAT.

Cattell, R.B. and Warburton, F.W. (1967). *Objective Personality and Motivation Tests*. Urbana, University of Illinois Press.

Cattell, R.B., Eber, H.W. and Tatsuoka, M.M. (1970a). *The 16-Factor Personality Questionnaire*. Champaign, IPAT.

Cattell, R.B., Horn, J.L. and Sweney, A.B. (1970b). *Motivation Analysis Test*. Champaign, IPAT.

Chapman, A.G. and Jones, D.G. (eds) (1980). *Models of Man*. Leicester, BPS.

Chopin, B.H. (1976). Recent developments in item banking. In de Gruijter, D.N.M. and van der Kamp, L.J.T. (1976).

Cliff, N. (1992). Abstract measurement theory and the revolution that never happened. *Psychological Science*, **3**, 186–190.

Cloninger, C.R. (1987). A systematic method for clinical description and classification of personality. *Archives of General Psychiatry*, **44**, 573–588.

Clyde, D. (1963). *Clyde Mood Scales*. Miami, University of Miami Press.

Conn, S.R. and Riecke, S.R. (1994). *The 16PF Fifth Edition Technical Manual*. Champaign, IPAT.

Cook, M. (1998). *Personnel Selection (3rd Edition)*. Chichester, Wiley.

Coombs, C.H., Daws, R.M. and Tversky, A. (1970). *Mathematical Psychology*. Englewood Cliffs, Prentice-Hall.

Cooper, C. and Kline, P. (1982). The internal structure of the Motivation Analysis Test. *British Journal of Educational Psychology*, **55**, 228–233.

Cooper, C. and McConnville, C. (1989) The factorial equivalence of the state-extraversion positive affect and state-anxiety negative affect. *Personality and Individual Differences*, **10**, 919–920.

Cooper, C. and Varma, V. (eds) (1997). *Processes in Individual Differences*. London, Routledge.

Cooper, C., Kline, P. and Maclaurin-Jones, C. (1986). Inspection time and primary abilities. *British Journal of Educational Psychology*, **56**, 304–308.

Cornwell, J.M. and Dunlap, W.P. (1994). On the questionable soundness of factoring ipsative data: a response to Saville and Wilson. *Journal of Occupational and Organisational Psychology*, **67**, 89–100.

Costa, P.T. and McCrae, R.R. (1988). From catalogue to classification: Murray's needs and the five factor model. *Journal of Personality and Social Psychology*, **55**, 258–265.

Costa, P.T. and McCrae, R.R. (1992a). *Revised NEO Personality Inventory (NEO-PI-R)*. Odessa, Psychological Assessment Resources.

Costa, P.T. and McCrae, R.R. (1992b). Four ways five factors are basic. *Personality and Individual Differences*, **13**, 653–665.

Costa, P.T., McCrae, R.R. and Holland, J.P. (1984). Personality and vocational interests in adulthood. *Journal of Applied Psychology*, **69**, 390–400.

Costa, P.T., Zondeman, A.B., Williams, R.B. and McCrae, R.R. (1985). Content and comprehensiveness in the MMPI: an item factor analysis in a normal adult sample. *Journal of Personality and Social Psychology*, **48**, 925–933.

Cronbach, L.J. (1946). Response sets and test validity. *Educational and Psychological Measurement*, **6**, 475–494.

Cronbach, L.J. (1951). Coefficient alpha and the internal structure of tests. *Psychometrika*, **16**, 297–334.

Cronbach, L.J. (1976). *Essentials of Psychological Testing*, third edition. New York, Harper & Row.

Cronbach, L.J. (1984). *Essentials of Psychological Testing*. New York, Harper and Row.

Cronbach, L.J (1994). *The Essentials of Psychological Testing* New York, HarperCollins.

Cronbach, L.J. and Meehl, P.E. (1955). Construct validity in psychological tests. *Psychological Bulletin*, **52**, 281–302.

Curran, J.P. and Cattell, R.B. (1974). *The Eight-State Questionnaire*. Champaign, IPAT.

Dahlstrom, W.G. and Welsh, G.S. (1960). *An MMPI Handbook*. London, Oxford University Press

Dawkins, R. (1976). *The Selfish Gene*. Oxford, Oxford University Press.

de Gruijter, D.N.M. and van der Kamp, L.J.T. (eds) (1976). *Advances in Educational and Psychological Measurement*. Chichester, Wiley.

Deary, I. and Caryl, P. (1993). Intelligence, EEG and evoked potentials. In Vernon, P.A. (ed.) (1993).

Deary, I.J. and Stough, C. (1996). Intelligence and inspection time: achievements, prospects and problems, *American Psychologist*, **51**, 599–608.

Deary, I.J., Egan, V., Gibson, D.J., Austin, E.J., Brand, C, and Kellagahan, T. (1996). Intelligence and the differentiation hypothesis. *Intelligence*, **23**, 105–122.

Digman, J.N. (1990). Personality structure: emergence of the five factor model. *Annual Review of Psychology*, **41**, 417–440.

Draycott, S.G. (1996). Investigations into psychometric measures and their prediction of human performance. PhD Thesis, University of Exeter.

Draycott, S.G. and Kline, P. (1994a). Further investigations into the nature of the BIP: a factor analysis of the BIP with primary abilities. *Personality and Individual Differences*, **17**, 201–209.

Draycott, S.G. and Kline, P. (1994b). Speed and ability: a research note. *Personality and Individual Differences*, **17**, 763–768.

Draycott, S.G. and Kline, P. (1995). The big three or the big five – the EPQ-R vs the NEO-PI: a research note and elaboration. *Personality and Individual Differences*, **18**, 801–804.

Draycott, S.G. and Kline, P. (1996). Validation of the AGARD STRES battery of performance tests. *Human Factors*, **38**, 347–371.

Eaves, L.W., Eysenck, H.J. and Martin, N.G. (1989). *Genes, Culture and Personality*. London, Academic Press.

Edwards, A.L. (1957). *The Social Desirability Variable in Personality Research*. New York, Dryden Press.

Ekstrom, R.B., French, J.W. and Harman, H.H. (1976). *Manual for Kit of Factor-Referenced Cognitive Tests*. New Jersey, Educational Testing Service.

Elliot, C. (1983). *The British Ability Scales.* Windsor, NFER.

Embretson, S.E. (1996). The new rules of measurement. *Psychological Assessment,* **8,** 341–349.

Ericsson, K.A. (1988). Analysis of memory performance in terms of memory skill. Chapter 5 in Sternberg, R.J. (1988).

Exner, J. (1986). *The Rorschach: A Comprehensive System.* New York, Wiley.

Eysenck, H.J. (1959). The Rorschach. In Buros, O.K. (1959).

Eysenck, H.J. (1967a). *The Biological Basis of Personality.* Springfield, C.C. Thomas.

Eysenck, H.J. (1967b). Intelligence assessment. A theoretical and experimental approach. *British Journal of Educational Psychology,* **37,** 81–98.

Eysenck, H.J. (1979). *The Structure and Measurement of Intelligence.* New York, Springer Verlag.

Eysenck, H.J. (ed.) (1982). *A Model for Intelligence.* New York, Springer.

Eysenck, H.J. (1985). *The Decline and Fall of the Freudian Empire.* Harmondsworth, Penguin Books.

Eysenck, H.J. (1986). Concluding chapter in Modgil, S. and Modgil, C. (eds) (1986).

Eysenck, H.J. (1992). Four ways five factors are not basic. *Personality and Individual Differences,* **13,** 667–673.

Eysenck, H.J. and Eysenck, S.G.B. (1975). *The Eysenck Personality Questionnaire.* Sevenoaks, Hodder and Stoughton.

Eysenck, H.J. and Eysenck, S.B.G. (1991). *The Eysenck Personality Scales.* Sevenoaks, Hodder and Stoughton.

Eysenck, H.J. and Eysenck, S.B.G. (1995). *Manual for the EPQ-R.* Sevenoaks, Hodder and Stoughton.

Fahrenberg, J. (1992). *Psychophysiology of Neuroticism and Anxiety.* In Gale, A.M. and Eysenck, M.W. (1992).

Ferguson, G.A. (1949). On the theory of test development. *Psychometrika,* **14,** 61–8.

Fisher, S. and Greenberg, R.P. (1995). *Freud Scientifically Reappraised.* New York, Wiley.

Frank, H. (1969). *Kybernetische Grundlagen der Pagadogik.* Bd 2. 2nd Agis edn, Baden-Baden.

Freud, S. (1908). Character and anal erotism. *S.E.,* 9, 169.

Freud, S. (1911). Psychoanalytic notes on an autobiographical account of a case of paranoia (dementia paranoides). *S.E.,* 12, 3.

Freud, S. (1923). *The Ego and the Id. S.E.,* 19, 3.

Freud, S. (1933). *New Introductory Lectures in Psychoanalysis. S.E.,* 22.

Freud, S. (1996). *Standard Edition of the Complete Psychological Works of Sigmund Freud.* London, Hogarth Press and Institute of Psychoanalysis.

Fulker, D.W. (1979). Nature and nurture: heredity. Chapter 5 in Eysenck, H.J. (1979).

Furnham, A. (1995). *Personality at Work.* London, Routledge.

Gale, A.M. and Eysenck, M.W. (eds) (1992). *Handbook of Individual Differences: Biological Perspectives.* Chichester, Wiley.

Gardner, H. (1983). *Frames of Mind: The Theory of Multiple Intelligences.* New York, Basic Books.

Ghiselli, E.E. (1966). *The Validity of Occupational Aptitude Tests.* New York, Wiley.

Goldberg, L.R. (1992). The development of markers for the big five factor structure. *Psychological Assessment,* **4,** 26–42.

Gorsuch, R.L. (1986). Measuring attitudes, interests, sentiments and values. 316–333 in Cattell, R.B. and Johnson, R.C. (1986).

Gottfredson, L.S. (1986) Societal consequences of the g factor in employment. *Journal of Vocational Behaviour*, **29**, 379–410.

Gottfredson, L.S. (1997a). Editorial. *Intelligence*, **24**, 1–12.

Gottfredson, L.S. (1997b). Why g matters: the complexity of everyday life. *Intelligence*, **24**, 79–132.

Gough, H.G. and Cook, M. (1997). *The California Personality Inventory*, fourth edition. Oxford, Oxford Psychologists Press.

Graham, J.R. (1990). *MMPI-2 Assessing Personality and Pathology*. New York, Oxford University Press.

Gregory, R.L. (1997). *Mirrors in Mind*. London, Penguin Books.

Grove, W.M. and Meehl, P.E. (1996). Comparative efficiency of informal (subjective, impressionistic) and formal (mechanical, algorithmic) prediction procedures. *Psychology. Public Policy and Law*, **2**, 292–323.

Guilford, J.P. (1959). *Personality*. New York, McGraw-Hill.

Guilford, J.P. (1964). Zero correlations among tests of intellectual abilities. *Psychological Bulletin*, **61**, 401–404.

Guilford, J.P. (1967). *The Nature of Human Intelligence*. New York, McGraw-Hill.

Guilford, J.P. and Hoepfner, R. (1971). *The Analysis of Intelligence*. New York, McGraw-Hill.

Haier, R.J. (1993). Cerebral glucose metabolism and intelligence. In Vernon, P.A. (ed.) (1993).

Hakstian A.R. and Cattell, R.B. (1976). *Manual for the Comprehensive Ability Battery*. Champaign, IPAT.

Hall, C.S. and Lindzey, G. (1966). *Theories of Personality*. New York, Wiley.

Hampson, S. and Kline, P. (1977). Personality dimensions differentiating certain groups of abnormal offenders from non-offenders. *British Journal of Criminology*, **17**, 310–331.

Harman, H.H. (1976). *Modern Factor Analysis*. Chicago, University of Chicago Press.

Hathaway, S.R. and McKinley, J.C. (1938). *The Minnesota Multiphasic Personality Inventory*. New York, Psychological Corporation.

Heim, A. (1975). *Psychological Testing*. London, Oxford University Press.

Heim, A.W., Watts, A.P. and Simmonds, V. (1970). *AH4, AH5, and AH6 Tests*. Windsor, NFER.

Hick, W. (1952). On the rate of gain of information. *Quarterly Journal of Experimental Psychology*, **4**, 11–26.

Holland, J.P. (1985a). *The Holland Vocational Preference Inventory (Revised)*. Odessa, Psychological Assessment Resources.

Holland, J.P. (1985b). *Making Career Choices: A Theory of Personality Types and Work Environments*. Englewood Cliffs, Prentice-Hall.

Holley, J.W. (1973). Rorschach analysis. 119–55 in Kline, P. (1973).

Horn, J. and Knapp, J.R. (1973). On the subjective character of the empirical base of Guilford's structure of intellect model. *Psychological Bulletin*, **80**, 33–43.

Howarth, E. (1976). Were Cattell's personality sphere factors correctly identified in the first instance? *British Journal of Psychology*, **67**, 213–230.

Howarth, E. (1980). *Technical Background and User Information for State and Trait Inventories*. Alberta, University of Alberta Press.

Hundleby, J.D. (1973). The measurement of personality by objective tests. 65–87 in Kline, P. (1973).

Jackson, D.N. (1974). *Personality Research Form*. New York, Research Psychologists Press.
Jackson, D.N. and Messick, S. (eds) (1967). *Problems in Human Assessment*. New York, Academic Press.
Jensen, A.R. (1980). *Bias in Mental Testing*. Glencoe, Free Press.
Jensen, A.R. (1987a). Individual differences on the Hick paradigm. In Vernon, P.A. (ed.) (1987).
Jensen, A.R. (1987b). The g beyond factor analysis. In Royce et al. (eds) (1987).
Jensen, A.R. (1994). Psychomtric g related to differences in head size. *Personality and Individual Differences*, 597–606.
Jensen, A.R. (1997). The neurophysiology of g. In Cooper, C. and Varma, V. (eds) (1997).
Jensen, A.R. (1998). *The g Factor: The Science of Mental Ability*. New York, Praeger.
Joreskog, K.G. and Sorbom, D. (1984). *LISREL, VI: Users' Guide* (3rd edition). Mooresville, Scientific Software.
Kanfer, R., Ackerman, P.L. Murtha, T. and Goff, M. (1995). Personality and intelligence in industrial and organisational psychology. 577–602 in Saklofske, D.H. and Zeidner, M. (1995).
Karon, B.P. (1981). *The Thematic Apperception Test*. 85–120 in Rabin, A.E. (1981).
Katz, M.R. (1972). The Strong Vocational Interest Blank. In Buros, O.K. (1972).
Kline, P. (1966). Extraversion, neuroticism and academic performance among Ghanaian university students. *British Journal of Educational Psychology*, **36**, 93–94.
Kline, P. (1971). *Ai3Q*. Windsor, NFER.
Kline, P. (ed.) (1973). *New Approaches in Psychological Measurement*. Chichester, Wiley.
Kline, P. (1979). *Psychometrics and Psychology*. London, Academic Press.
Kline, P. (1980). The psychometric model. In Chapman, A.G. and Jones, D.M. (eds) (1980).
Kline, P. (1981). *Fact and Fantasy in Freudian Theory* (2nd edn). London, Methuen.
Kline, P. (1986). *Handbook of Test Construction*. London, Methuen (now Routledge).
Kline, P. (1991). *Intelligence: The Psychometric View*. London, Routledge.
Kline, P. (1993). *The Handbook of Psychological Testing*. London, Routledge.
Kline, P. (1994). *An Easy Guide to Factor Analysis*. London, Routledge.
Kline, P. (1998). *The New Psychometrics*. London, Routledge.
Kline, P. (1999). *The Handbook of Psychological Testing* (2nd edn). London, Routledge.
Kline, P. and Barrett, P. (1983). The factors in personality questionnaires among normal subjects. *Advances in Behaviour Research and Therapy*, 141–202.
Kline, P. and Cooper, C. (1984a). The factor structure of the Comprehensive Ability Battery. *British Journal of Educational Psychology*, **54**, 106–110.
Kline, P. and Cooper, C. (1984b). A construct validation of the Object Analytic Test Battery (OATB). *Personality and Individual Differences*, **5**, 328–337.
Kline, P. and Cooper, C. (1984c). A factorial analysis of the authoritarian character. *British Journal of Psychology*, **75**, 171–176.
Kline, P. and Grindley, J. (1974). A 28-day case study of the MAT. *Journal of Multivariate Experimental Personality Clinical Psychology*, 1, 13–32.
Kline, P., Draycott, S.G. and McAndrew, V.M. (1994). Reconstructing intelligence: a factor analytic study of the BIP. *Personality and Individual Differences*, **16**, 529–536.
Klopfer, B. and Kelley, D.M. (1942). *The Rorschach Technique*. Tarrytown-on-Hudson, World Book Co.

Kranzler, J.H. (1990). The nature of intelligence: A unitary process or a number of processes: Unpublished doctoral dissertation, University of California at Berkeley.

Krug, S.E. (1980). *Clinical Analysis Questionnaire*. Champaign, IPAT.

Krug, S.E. (1986). Solid-state psychology: the role of the computer in human assessment. 127–114 in Cattell, R.B. and Johnson, R.C. (1986).

Krug, S.E. and Johns, E.F. (1986). A large-scale cross-validation of second order personality structure as defined by the 16PF. *Psychological Reports*, **59**, 683–693.

Kuder, G.F. (1970a). *Kuder General Interest Survey*. Chicago, Science Research Associates.

Kuder, G.F. (1970b). *Kuder Occupational Interests Survey*. Chicago, Science Research Associates.

Kyllonen, P.C. (1985). *Dimensions of Information Processing*. Brooks Air Force Base, Texas, Air Force Systems Command.

Kyllonen, P.C. and Christal, R.E. (1990). Reasoning ability is (little more than) working memory capacity. *Intelligence*, **14**, 389–433.

Lehrl, S. and Fischer, B. (1990). A basic information psychological parameter (BIP) for the reconstruction of the concepts of intelligence. *European Journal of Personality*, **4**, 259–286.

Levy, P. (1973). On the relation of test theory and psychology. In Kline, P. (1973).

Likert, R.A. (1932). A technique for the measurement of attitudes. *Archives of Psychology*, No. 140.

Livesley, W.J., Jackson, D.N. and Schroeder, M.L. (1992). *Journal of Abnormal Psychology*, **101**, 432–440.

Lochlin, J.C. (1987). *Latent Variable Models*. Hillsdale, Erlbaum.

Lord, F.M. (1974). *Individualised Testing and Item Response Theory*. Princeton, ETS.

Luce, R.D. and Tukey, J.W. (1964). Simultaneous conjoint measurement: a new type of fundamental measurement. *Journal of Mathematical Psychology*, **1**, 1–27.

Mackintosh, N.J. (1986). The biology of intelligence? *British Journal of Psychology*, **77**, 1–18.

Mackintosh, N.J. (1998). *Intelligence*. Cambridge, Cambridge University Press

Mathews, G. and Deary, I.J. (1998). *Personality Traits*. Cambridge, Cambridge University Press.

McCormick, E.J., Jeanneret, P.R. and Mecahm, R.C. (1972). A study of job characteristics and job dimensions as based on the Position Analysis Questionnaire (PAQ). *Journal of Applied Psychology*, **56**, 347–368.

McCrae, R.R. and Costa, P.T. (1989). Reinterpreting the Myers–Briggs Type Indicator from the perspective of the five factor model of personality. *Journal of Personality*, **57**, 17–40.

McDougall, W. (1932). *The Energies of Men*. London. Methuen.

Meyer, G.J. and Shack, J.R. (1989). Structural convergence of mood and personality: evidence for old and new directions. *Journal of Personality and Social Psychology*, **57**, 670–691.

Michell, J. (1990). *An Introduction to the Logic of Psychological Measurement*. Hillsdale, Erlbaum.

Michell, J. (1997). Quantitative science and the definition of measurement in psychology. *British Journal of Psychology*, **88**, 355–383.

Miller, E.M. (1994). Intelligence and brain myelination: a hypothesis. *Personality and Individual Differences*, **17**, 803–832.

Millon, T. (1983). *Millon Clinical Multiaxial Inventory*. Minneapolis, Interpretative Scoring Systems.

Modgil, S. and Modgil, C. (eds) (1986). *Hans Eysenck: Consensus and Controversy*. Lewes, Falmar Press.

Murray, H.A. (1938). *Explorations in Personality*. New York, Oxford University Press.

Murray, H.A. (1971). *The Thematic Apperception Test*. Boston, Harvard University Press.

Nunnally, J. O. (1978). *Psychometric Theory*. New York, McGraw Hill.

Nunnally, J.O. and Bernstein, I.H. (1994). *Psychometric Theory*. New York, McGraw-Hill.

Otis, A.S. (1954). *Quick Scoring Ability Tests*. London, Harrap.

Pedersen, N.L., Plomin, R., Nesselroade, J.R. and McClearn, G.E. (1992). *Psychological Science*, **3**, 346–352.

Pedley, R.R. (1955). *The Comprehensive School*. Harmondsworth, Penguin.

Pervin, L. (ed.) (1990). *Handbook of Personality Theory and Research*. New York, Guilford Press.

Petrill, S., Plomin, R., McGlearn, G.E. and Smith, D.L. (1996). DNA markers associated with general and specific cognitive abilities. *Intelligence*, **23**, 191–203.

Piedmont, R.L., McCrae, R.R. and Costa, P.T. (1991). Adjective check list scales and the five factor model of personality. *Journal of Personality and Social Psychology*, **60**, 630–637.

Plomin, R. and Petril, S. (1997). Genetics and intelligence: what's new? *Intelligence*, **24**, 53–77.

Plomin, S.A. et al. (1998). Failure to replicate a QTL association between a DNA marker identified by EST00083 and IQ. *Intelligence*, **25**, 179–184.

Popper, K. (1959). *The Logic of Scientific Discovery*. New York, Basic Books.

Posner, M.I. (1978). *Chronometric Explorations of Mind*. Hillsdale, Erlbaum.

Rabin, A.E. (ed.) (1981). *Assessment with Projective Techniques*. New York, Springer.

Rasch, G. (1960). *Probabilistic Models for Some Attainment and Intelligence Tests*. Copenhagen, Denmark Institute of Education.

Raven, J.C. (1965a). *Progressive Matrices*. London, H.K. Lewis.

Raven, J.C. (1965b). *The Crichton Vocabulary Scale*. London, H.K. Lewis.

Raven, J.C. (1965c). *The Mill–Hill Vocabulary Scale*. London, H.K. Lewis.

Reeves, D.L., Winter, K.P., LaCour, S.J., Raynsford, K.M., Vogel, K. and Grisset, J.D. (1991). The UTC-PAB/AGARD STRES battery: user's manual and systems documentation. Pensacole. Naval Aerospace Medical Research Laboratory.

Roberts, R.D. (1997). The factor structure of reaction times (RT) and their relationships to intelligence. Paper at the Second Spearman Conference, July 1997. Plymouth, Devon.

Roberts, R.D., Pallier, G. and Stankov, R. (1996). The basic information processing (BIP) unit, mental speed and human cognitive abilities: should the BIP R.I.P.? *Intelligence*, **23**, 133–155.

Robinson, D.L. (1999). The 'IQ' factor: implications for intelligence theory and measurement. *Personality and Individual Differences* (in press).

Robinson, J.P., Shaver, P.R. and Wrightsman, L.S. (eds) (1991). *Measures of Personality and Social Psychological Attitudes*. New York, Academic Press.

Rokeach, M. (1960). *The Open and Closed Mind*. New York, Basic Books.

Rorschach, H. (1921). *Psychodiagnostics*. Berne, Hans Huber.

Roskam, E.E. (ed.) (1994). *Measurement in Personality Assessment*. Amsterdam, Elsevier.

Royce, R.R. (1967). Factors as theoretical constructs. In Jackson, D.N. and Messick, S. (eds) (1967).

Royce, R.R., Glover, J.A. and Witt, J.C. (eds) (1987). *The Influence of Cognitive Psychology on Testing*. Hillsdale, Erlbaum.

Rushton, J.P. and Ankney, C.D. (1996). Brain size and cognitive ability: correlations with age, sex, social class and race. *Psychonomic Bulletin and Review*, **3**, 21–36.

Saklofske, D.H. and Zeidner, M. (eds) (1995). *The International Handbook of Personality and Intelligence*. New York, Plenum.

Salgado, J.F. (1997). The five factor model of personality and job performance in the European community. *Journal of Applied Psychology*, **82**, 30–43.

Schmidt, F.L. and Hunter, J.E. (1998). The validity and utility of selection methods in personnel psychology: practical and theoretical implications of 85 years of research findings. *Psychological Bulletin*, **124**, 261–274.

Schonnell, F.J. and Schonnell, F.E. (1950). *Diagnostic and Attainment Testing*. Edinburgh, Oliver and Boyd.

Schroeder, M.I., Wormsworth, J.R. and Liveley, W.J. (1992). Dimensions of personality disorder and their relationship to the big five dimensions of personality. *Psychological Assessment*, **4**, 47–53.

Seashore, C.E. (1919). *The Psychology of Musical Talent*. New York, Burdett.

Skinner, B.F. (1953). *Science and Human Behaviour*. New York, Macmillan.

Skuder, P. et al. (1995). A polymorphism in mitochondrial DNA associated with IQ. *Intelligence*, **21**, 1–12.

Smith, M. and Robertson, I. (eds) (1989). *Advances in Selection and Assessment*. Chichester, Wiley.

Spearman, C. (1904). 'General intelligence': objectively determined and measured. *American Journal of Psychology*, **15**, 201–292.

Spielberger, C.D., Gorsuch, D.L. and Lushene, R.E. (1970). *Manual for the State–Trait Anxiety Inventory*. Palo Alto, Consulting Psychologists Press.

Stankov, S., Boyle, G.J. and Cattell, R.B. (1995) Models and paradigms in personality and intelligence research. In Saklofske, D.H. and Zeidner, M. (eds) (1995).

Stelmack, R.M. and Geen, R.G. (1992). The psychophysiology of extraversion. In Gale, A.M. and Eysenck, M.W. (1992).

Stelmack, R.M. and Houlihan, R.M. (1995). Event-related potentials, personality and intelligence: concepts, issues and evidence. In Saklofske, D.H. and Zeidner, M. (1992).

Sternberg, R.J. (ed.) 1988). *Advances in the Psychology of Human Intelligence Vol. 4*. Hillsdale, Erlbaum.

Sternberg, S. (1969). Memory scanning: mental processes revealed by reaction time experiments. *American Scientist*, **57**, 421–457.

Stevens, S.S. (1946). On the theory of scales of measurement. *Science*, **103**, 667–680.

Stevens, S.S. (1951). Mathematics, measurement and psychophysics. In Stevens, S.S. (ed.) (1951). *Handbook of Experimental Psychology*. New York, Wiley.

Strong, E.K. (1927). A vocational interest test. *The Educational Record*, **8**, 107–121.

Strong, E.K. and Campbell, D.P. (1974). *Strong–Campbell Interest Inventory* (Revised edn). Stanford, Stanford University Press.

Strong, E.K., Campbell, D.P., Berdie, R.E. and Clerk, K.E. (1971). *Strong Vocational Interest Blank*. Stanford, Stanford University Press.

Sweney, A.B. and Cattell, R.B. (1980). *Manual for the Vocational Interest Measure*. Champaign, IPAT.

Sweney, A.B., Anton, M.T. and Cattell, R.B. (1986). Evaluating motivation structure, conflict and adjustment. In Cattell, R.B. and Johnson, R.C. (1986).

Terman, L.M. and Oden, M. (1959). *The Gifted Group at Mid-Life.* Stanford, California University Press.

Thurstone, L.L. (1947). *Multiple Factor Analysis: A Development and Expansion of Vectors of the Mind.* Chicago, University of Chicago Press.

Undheim, J.O. (1981). On Intelligence 2. A neo-Spearmanian model to replace Cattell's theory of fluid and crystallised intelligence. *Scandinavian Journal of Psychology,* **22**, 181–187.

Undheim, J.O. and Gustafsson, J.E. (1987). The hierarchical organisation of cognitive abilities: restoring general intelligence through the use of linear structure relations (LISREL). *Multivariate Behavioural Research,* **22**, 149–171.

Vernon, P.A. (ed.) (1987). *Speed of Information Processing and Intelligence.* Norwood, N.J., Ablex.

Vernon, P.A. (ed.) (1993). *Biological Approaches to the Study of Human Intelligence.* Norwood, N.J., Ablex.

Vernon, P.E. (1961). *The Measurement of Abilities.* London, University of London Press.

Vernon, P.E. (1963). *Personality Assessment.* London, Methuen.

Vickers, D., Pietch, A. and Hemingway, T. (1995). The frequency accrual speed test, FAST: a new measure of mental speed. *Personality and Individual Differences,* **19**, 863–879.

Vigil-Colet, A., Perez-Olle, J. and Fernandez, M. (1997). The relationship of basic information processing measures with fluid and crystallised intelligence. *Personality and Individual Differences,* **23**, 55–65.

Warburton, F.W. (1965). Observations on a sample of psychopathic American criminals. *Behaviour Research Therapy,* **3**, 129–135.

Watson, D. (1988). Vicissitudes of mood measurement: effects of varying descriptions, time-frames, and response formats on measures of positive and negative affect. *Journal of Personality and Social Psychology,* **55**, 128–141.

Watson, D. and Tellegen, A. (1985). Towards a consensual structure of mood. *Psychological Bulletin,* **98**, 219–235.

Webster, R. (1995). *Why Freud was Wrong.* London, HarperCollins.

Wechsler, D. (1958). *The Measurement and Appraisal of Adult Intelligence* (4th edn). Baltimore, Williams and Wilkins.

Whurr, R. (1996). *Aphasic Screening Test* (2nd edn). London, Whurr Publishing.

Widiger, T.A. and Costa, P.T. (1994). Personality and personality disorders. *Journal of Abnormal Psychology,* **103**, 78–91.

Woliver, R.E. and Saeks, S.D. (1986). Intelligence and primary aptitude: test design and tests available. In Cattell, R.B. and Johnson, R.C. (1986).

Wood, R. (1978). Fitting the Rasch model: a heady tale. *British Journal of Mathematical and Statistical Psychology,* **31**, 27–32.

Wright, B.D. (1985). Additivity in psychological measurement. In Roskam, E.E. (1985).

Zimmerman, D.W. and Williams, R.H. (1998). Reliability of gain scores under realistic assumptions about properties of pre-test and post-test scores. *British Journal of Mathematical and Statistical Psychology,* **51**, 343–351.

Index

Compiled by Sue Carlton